William Temple (1881–1944) was the outstanding British religious leader of this century. He believed that the 'modern state' was incomplete without a modern Christian church, which should set the moral and political tone of the community. His political and religious best-seller, *Christianity and Social Order*, which was published as a Penguin Special in 1942, was one of the sources of the wide support for the British Welfare State of the 1950s. Temple was the most successful and controversial of British 'priests in politics', because as an Archbishop he combined the idea of a national unity rooted in a common set of religious/moral values with a constant demand for political change in the direction of greater social equality. He thus combined conservative and radical impulses to a remarkable degree.

This is a study of Temple's public life and policy in Britain, and of his part in the movement to unite the world's Protestant churches. At a time of difficulty for the Church of England, when its role in national life is under threat and national unity is difficult to achieve in a plural society, Temple's career as the last great articulate exponent of Anglicanism calls for a fresh assessment.

BRITISH LIVES

# William Temple

# BRITISH LIVES

Edited by Maurice Cowling
*Fellow of Peterhouse, Cambridge*

and John Vincent
*Professor of History, University of Bristol*

This is a series of short, scholarly biographical studies which will address the lives of major figures from the early medieval period to modern times. Each figure will be of political, intellectual or religious significance in British or British imperial history. A major aim of the series is to seek out and scrutinise figures whose current interpretation has become stale or conventional, and to establish a lively interaction between author and subject in an attempt to place each historical figure in a new light.

# William Temple

Church, state and
society in Britain,
1880–1950

JOHN KENT

Emeritus Professor of Theology
University of Bristol

CAMBRIDGE
UNIVERSITY PRESS

Published by the Press Syndicate of the University of Cambridge
The Pitt Building, Trumpington Street, Cambridge CB2 1RP
40 West 20th Street, New York, NY10011–4211, USA
10 Stamford Road, Oakleigh, Victoria 3166, Australia

First published 1992

Printed in Great Britain by Redwood Press Ltd, Melksham, Wiltshire

*A catalogue record for this book is available from the British Library*

*Library of Congress cataloguing in publication data*
Kent, John, 1923–
William Temple:church, state and society in Britain, 1880–1950
/ John Kent.
p.   cm. – (British lives)
Includes bibliographical references and index.
ISBN 0 521 37484 7 – ISBN 0 521 37630 0 (pbk.)
1. Temple, William, 1881–1944.   I. Title.   II. Series.
BX5199.   T42K46   1992
283'.092 – dc20   91-44742   CIP
[B]

ISBN 0 521 37484 7 hardback
ISBN 0 521 37630 0 paperback

# Contents

| | | |
|---|---|---|
| Preface | | page ix |
| Chronology | | xii |
| | INTRODUCTION | 1 |
| 1 | TEMPLE'S CAREER | 9 |
| 2 | MODERNISING THE CHURCH | 33 |
| | Temple's theological writings | 38 |
| | Life and Liberty | 61 |
| | The Ecumenical Movement | 95 |
| 3 | THE CHURCH IN POLITICS | 115 |
| | Copec | 115 |
| | The General Strike 1926 | 135 |
| | The Malvern Conference 1941 | 148 |
| 4 | A REASSESSMENT | 168 |
| | References | 191 |
| | Index | 195 |

# Preface

William Temple, one of the most remarkable Christian leaders of the twentieth century, has not been much studied since his death in 1944, and it is time that his career was reassessed. He set out during the First World War to modernise the institutions and liberalise the theological attitudes of the Church of England; between the wars he more than anyone else worked to create a new international unity out of the mainstream Protestant churches; throughout his career he tried to persuade Anglicans to act politically on the side of greater social equality. These aims constituted a public religious policy, which he hoped would justify the existence of an established church in England and foster a national unity based on a religious, specifically Christian, outlook. Temple was not so much inventing as seeking to renew a version of 'English' history which was already struggling for credibility by 1920. He could perhaps be understood as editing in an urban direction the pastoral English nationalism which Stanley Baldwin integrated into Conservatism in the 1920s and 1930s. He was seeking to reclaim religious authority over a society which had become predominantly secular, and this meant that politicians frequently criticised him. His was a public religious career of an unusual kind, perhaps the last of its kind possible in England, and it needs a fresh evalution.

The existing literature of Temple does not provide what is needed. An official biography by one of Temple's old associates, F. A. Iremonger, *William Temple Archbishop of Canterbury: His Life and Letters* (Oxford, Oxford University Press, 1948), is too detailed to be easily replaced, but too close to Temple to examine him in his historical context. Much of the correspondence on which Iremonger worked is now in Lambeth Palace Library. Some years later, F. S. Temple edited *Some Lambeth Letters 1942–1944* (Oxford, Oxford University Press, 1963), a useful selection of William Temple's correspondence as Archbishop of Canterbury. Attempts were made in the 1960s to re-examine Temple's theology, the most informative of these being Joseph Fletcher's *William Temple: Twentieth-Century Christian* (New York, Seabury Press, 1963), although the best critical analysis of his philosophy is J. F. Padgett's *The Christian Philosophy of William Temple* (The Hague, M. Nijhoff, 1974). In the mean time political enthusiasm was shifting from left to right, so that when in 1976 Temple's political best-seller, *Christianity and Social Order*, which had been published originally as a Penguin Special in 1942, was reissued by Shepheard-Walwyn/SPCK with a long introduction by Professor R. H. Preston of Manchester, no revival of interest followed. Those who thought that religion should confine itself to the inner life of the individual often became openly critical of Temple: see, for example, E. R. Norman, in *Church and Society in England 1770–1970* (Oxford, Clarendon Press, 1976); and more recently Corelli Barnett, whose polemic, *The Audit of War* (London, Macmillan, 1986), includes Temple among those whose debilitating Christian influence helped to prevent a full British economic recovery after the Second World War. A. M. Suggate's recent *William Temple and Christian Social Ethics Today* (Edinburgh, Clark, 1987) is primarily an essay in contemporary theology.

This book is chiefly based on the Lambeth Palace documents and Temple's writings, including his journalism. It fits into the literature as a reinterpretation of Temple's career. There was nothing enigmatic about the man: his religious style was mild but firm, his character not inappropriately unsophisticated, though the absence of worldliness could in some fields amount to a lack of insight, and his mind was deeply invaded by Edwardian images of England as the ultimate imperial power. What I am concerned with here, however, is a tradition of cooperation and conflict in public policy between state, church and community. Temple both represented and significantly modified an Anglican interpretation of England which had once been powerful. His efforts to sustain not only the Church of England but also English Christianity in a central political role are of great interest.

I should like to acknowledge the great help given me by the librarians at Lambeth Palace Library. I am also indebted to the staff at the Bodleian Library, Oxford, at Bristol University Library and at the Library of Bristol Baptist College. I am very grateful to my editors, Maurice Cowling and John Vincent, for their kindness and criticisms: they bear no responsibility for my conclusions. I must also thank Bishop F. S. Temple for answering my questions; Dr Haddon Willmer, not least for the loan of books; and the Christendom Trust, through which I first came to write on William Temple. Anyone who works in this field is bound to be stimulated by the writing of Adrian Hastings and E. R. Norman; I have also learned from Duncan Forrester, whose doubts about 'middle axioms' I share. My biggest debt, however, is to my wife: *cor ad cor loquitur*.

# Chronology

| | |
|---|---|
| 1881 | William Temple born, 15 October, at Exeter. |
| 1900 | Balliol College, Oxford |
| 1904 | Fellow of Queen's College, Oxford |
| 1905 | Joined the Workers' Educational Association: President 1908–24 |
| 1909 | After lengthy negotiation, ordained by the Archbishop of Canterbury |
| 1910 | *The Faith and Modern Thought* |
| | Attended the Edinburgh World Missionary Conference |
| | Visited Australia for the SCM |
| | Headmaster of Repton |
| 1912 | Contributed to *Foundations: A Statement of Christian Belief*, by Seven Oxford Men |
| 1914 | Rector of St James's, Piccadilly, London |
| 1915 | His mother died, 2 April |
| | Edited *Challenge* until 1918 |
| 1916 | Married Frances Anson, 24 June |
| | Member of Archbishops' Commission on Church and State |
| 1917 | *Mens Creatrix* |
| | Life and Liberty movement began, 16 July |
| | Resigned St James's, Piccadilly |
| 1919 | The Enabling Act |
| 1920–7 | Edited the *Pilgrim* |

# Chronology

| | |
|---|---|
| 1921 | Bishop of Manchester |
| 1923 | Member and from 1925 Chairman, of the Archbishops' Commission on Christian Doctrine |
| 1924 | *Christus Veritas* |
| | Copec met at Birmingham |
| 1926 | The General Strike and the miners' strike |
| 1929 | Archbishop of York |
| | Chairman of Faith and Order |
| 1934 | *Nature, Man and God* |
| 1937 | Chairman of the Edinburgh Faith and Order Conference |
| 1938 | Published the report *Doctrine in the Church of England* |
| 1939–40 | The 'Lansdowne' Letter and the Zilven Meeting |
| 1941 | The Malvern Conference |
| 1942 | *Christianity and Social Order* (the Penguin Special) |
| | Archbishop of Canterbury |
| 1944 | Died at Westgate, 26 October |

# Introduction

William Temple, who died as Archbishop of Canterbury in 1944, was the outstanding religious figure in Britain in the twentieth century. He was one of the most effective advocates of the British Welfare State. He more than anyone else formed a new international religious body – the World Council of Churches – out of mainstream Protestantism and Orthodoxy. He thought that the modern state needed a modernised state church to help foster national unity on the basis of common ethical and religious standards. He strove with some success to modernise the institutions and liberalise the theology of the Church of England, and he believed that his overall policies would justify the continued existence of an English state church linked to the monarchy. If the Church of England, contrary to much Victorian expectation, has survived into the 1990s, and still sometimes acts as though being 'established' means defining the moral limits of government policies, it is because Temple gave fresh life to the vision of a partnership between church and state.

When Temple was born in 1881 the Church of England seemed to be losing a long struggle to preserve any significant social and political power. The Free churches and the Roman Catholic Church were challenging its central position in the nation's life. The state had recently set up a national system of popular education which was largely free from ecclesiastical authority. Even in Oxford, Christian theology was losing its grip on the intellectual imagination and declining into the concern of a religious sub-culture. The vast majority of the Anglican clergy served their parishes well, this religious decline differing from those of the past inasmuch as it could not be blamed on a lack of faith, hard work and charity in the priesthood. At the political level, Anglicanism added pious approval to the dominant politics of the day, as when late Victorian bishops described the hand of God in the growth of the British Empire, but that approval no longer counted for very much.

Temple did not altogether reject that view of the Empire, any more than he rejected the institution of establishment, but he recognised that in the twentieth century the Church of England had to justify itself all over again in religious and political terms if it was to survive. He believed that the state church could do what no other social institution could do: it could bind the English people together in a common faith in shared values, and in doing so perform a vital religious and political service. However deeply a modern society was divided by differences of class, wealth and belief – and these differences were only too obvious in the England of 1914, let alone 1939 – and however secular its culture had become, it still needed to resist chaos by finding a common identity and becoming a community. Temple did not deny the existence of what is now called pluralism, but he denied that it was an end in itself: social health also required a set of common values. At first sight, Temple was reviving a seventeenth-century theory of the proper relationship between church and state, in which the church left politics to the politicians and concentrated on the moral education of the nation. In practice, Temple went further, because he was unwilling to leave the political arena entirely to what was becoming a secular state.

To carry out such a programme the establishment had to be changed. The Church of England had to be freed as far as possible from Parliament's control of its liturgy and doctrine, and a more democratic form of self-government had to be introduced to spread power wider than the priesthood. There had to be an end of Anglican introspection: theologians should leave Victorian doubt to the Victorians and recognise that in the wider world modern thought was moving towards theism, even, Temple claimed, Christian theism, and not away from it. Above all, the Church of England had to adopt an openly critical social role, involving a campaign for greater social and economic equality. Some nineteenth-century Anglicans had criticised the development of Victorian industrial society on theological grounds, but Temple knew that these critics had achieved very little. He wanted a more effective approach, and he achieved it so well that one of his sharpest critics called him 'the most conspicuous of all clergymen in promoting the vision of a New Jerusalem' (Barnett, 1986, p. 15). He gradually changed the old establishment into an institution whose criticisms of government policy could not simply be ignored.

There were many obstacles to Temple's success. The majority of the urban working class, for example, did not belong either to the Church of England or to other religious bodies: they were wary of concepts of 'national unity'. Temple's immediate resource, the Anglican priesthood, often seemed more interested in internal Anglican politics than in the social problems of the world outside the church. The religious excitement generated by the conflicts between Anglo-Catholics and Anglican Evangelicals in the 1920s reassured their consciences, while in the 1930s horror at the idea of approaching war made pacifism a major public issue among them. The priesthood were accustomed to a kind of public moralising – about drink, gambling and sexual behaviour, for example – which had no drastic political consequences: they were less enthusiastic about what seemed to them direct political commitment. As for the Anglican laity, when Temple tried to draw the religious section of the English middle classes out of privacy into politics through an Anglican programme of social change, he found himself competing with the Conservative leader, Stanley Baldwin, who offered them his own secular variety of pastoral English nationalism. Yet Baldwin's desire to make the Conservative Party the focus of national unity was itself in part a response to persistent Anglican self-questioning about the morality of industrial society.

Temple was seeking political influence, and it is arguable that in a democratic society a religious group which seeks to intervene in politics should form a political party, as has been done in Europe since the late nineteenth century, and accept the verdict of the electorate. In the 1920s this course was not open to Temple, because it would have broken the accepted rules of British political behaviour. His solution was to construct a powerful pressure-group inside the churches which would advocate his social programme. He did this first in the 1920s and again in the 1940s, when the controversy about what the war was being fought for – apart from the defeat of Hitler – gave him a fresh opportunity to press his views. His success in making the concept of greater social equality more respectable in middle-class religious circles remained a solid contribution to the setting-up of the British Welfare State after the Second World War. He compelled the Church of England, above all in the 1940s, to re-examine its relationship to British politics, and in doing so he bridged the gap between Victorian Anglicanism and an Anglicanism which will survive into the next century. He created a modern tradition of Anglican political interventionism which was sustained by later Archbishops, notably Michael Ramsey and Robert Runcie. Temple saw that Anglicanism was an endangered species; he concluded that it would last longer if it acted dangerously.

Temple's attitude contradicted that of the inter-war Anglican Primates, Davidson and Lang, both of whom thought that the Church of England should concentrate on reducing its internal divisions and should risk attracting political attention only in highly abnormal circumstances – as Davidson did in the General Strike and as Lang did when Edward VIII abdicated. Temple rejected these limits on the state church's political involvement and argued that Anglicanism ought to have its own programme of social reform and ought to campaign for it steadily. In so far as this applied to foreign affairs as well, he and Lang were closer together in theory, though once again Lang was reluctant to enter the political arena. Both had hoped that the League of Nations could become the instrument of a Christian peace-movement, both reacted to the crises of the 1930s by feeling that the churches must, by the very nature of the religion they taught, try to preserve peace until the last possible moment, and Temple, as we shall see, applied that principle with characteristic boldness even in 1940. Neither was a pacifist, and Temple was tougher in his dismissal of pacifism as a Christian option. They were both willing to believe that the church was a community which could release spiritual power into the most desperate human situations. If the peace settlement after the Second World War was more successful than Versailles, perhaps it owed something to the steadiness with which, during the war, Temple and others criticised any doctrine of unconditional surrender which might lead to a destructive peace treaty.

His awareness that the churches, including the Church of Rome, carried little or no weight in international affairs was a major reason why Temple pursued church unity with such passion – he claimed in 1943 that the churches were united internationally at the very moment when the secular world was falling apart. The World Council of Churches, of which he was the first official leader, was not in his mind a 'superchurch' or an alternative Vatican. But just as he believed that the Church of England was entitled to offer what amounted to political guidance to the British government of the day, so he believed that the World Council of Churches provided the non-Roman Catholic churches with a way of transcending their local national limits and of playing a creative role on the world stage. Since his death the World Council has grown in size, but has not produced another leader of his international stature.

Temple has been criticised on various grounds, but most importantly by Corelli Barnett in *The Audit of War* (1986). Barnett's fundamental assumption was that in 1945 Britain had preferred the self-indulgence of a welfare state ('The New Jerusalem') which it could not afford to the austerity which would have established the basis of a strong economic recovery. Temple was a prominent example of those who had lured the British into making the wrong decision, and so he was one of those responsible for Britain's postwar decline. His Oxford education had left out 'anything to do with understanding the modern world or Britain's place in it'. The conference which he organised at Malvern in 1941 on postwar reconstruction 'was one of the first and most effective gambits in launching the New Jerusalem movement' (Barnett, 1986, p. 16). As far as Barnett was concerned, Temple's appeal to religious sentiment only added a fatal attractiveness to a political misjudgement.

Barnett's case was weak at its initial point: in 1945 social reform and economic reconstruction were not alternatives. He himself virtually admits that in 1945 many politicians on the right as well as the left recognised the inevitability of at least some of what he calls the New Jerusalem policies, the ideas which Beveridge had put forward during the war. It is too easy, however, to explain this in terms of a New Jerusalem movement which preferred sentiment to business efficiency. The irresistible demand for change was secular: its origin was a widespread feeling that the British people, having had to fight in 1914 and again in 1939, expected changes in return. Temple no doubt shared that feeling, and added to it the conviction that fairness, if not exactly equality, was inherent in the attitude of the Jesus of the gospels. He reinforced the secular enthusiasm for some kind of welfare state with his own vision of a New Jerusalem. If he made a mistake, what he got wrong was the religion rather than the politics.

Temple's importance did not lie in his personal life, which was that of a quiet, happily married, perhaps over-confident man, whose great energy flowed endlessly into an episcopal public persona, but in these ideas and their relationship to the historical period stretching from the 1850s to the present day. In those years the position of Christianity in Western culture deteriorated steadily. The kind of problems which Anglicanism faced were very similar to those faced by the Christian churches in Europe. There were two broad 'Christian' reactions to this decline. The first and earlier (which was also Temple's) was to reassert that Christianity had been and must continue to be at the centre of Western culture, a view still held by Pope John Paul II. The second, which developed strongly from the 1920s, was to give up the idea of a Christian hegemony in the West but to argue that the business of the church was to witness to a final vindication of the truth of Christianity in a divine judgement. Those who took the second view were apt to think of themselves as more 'orthodox' than those who took the first, and their attitude should be distinguished from the later 'liberal' view (from the 1970s) that the time had gone when any religious group should seriously think of claiming cultural hegemony in what was developing into a global society. It has been adherents of the second position who have written most of the studies of Temple's career, and those in the third who should be able to appreciate what he achieved. He is more than due for reappraisal.

# Chapter 1

# Temple's career

Temple's attitude to the Church of England, which seems to have defined his horizons almost entirely for much of his life, was a function of his background. His father, Frederick, then Bishop of Exeter, had been fifty-five when he married in 1876, and was nearly sixty when William, his younger son, was born. His mother, Beatrice Lascelles, though much younger than her husband, was thirty-six at William's birth. There was a certain similarity between father and son where marriage was concerned. Frederick Temple's mother had died in 1866, when he was forty-five, and he had finally married ten years later. William's mother died in 1915, and he married Frances Anson in 1916, when he was thirty-five: there were no children.

Before William was four years old his father at last entered, as Bishop of London, the inner circle of the Anglican episcopate. William grew up in what was essentially a public household, with a mother whose personal connexions were aristocratic (her father was a younger son of the Earl of Harewood and her mother a daughter of the Earl of Carlisle) and a father whose whole existence symbolised public religious authority. Frederick Temple became Archbishop of Canterbury in 1896, while William was still at school. Frederick Temple may not always have accepted the limits of traditional dogmatic Christianity, but there was no question of his playing down the possibilities of his role as Archbishop. From Lambeth Palace one can see the Palace of Westminster across the water, and an Archbishop's freedom to use the political theatre and social club of the House of Lords was still a central part of his day-to-day activity.

Temple's was a childhood completely enveloped in an upper-class Anglican culture which still believed itself to be a permanent, necessary part of an English society which would lose its essential character if it were not Anglican, a childhood lived in a London which was now briefly a world capital, the heart of an empire on which the sun had not yet set. It was to give him a feeling, which he never lost, that the Church of England, properly organised, could give reality to the assertion that this was a Christian country, and that it could also become the driving-force in a world church, a transcendent version of the British Empire. He was accustomed to see the world from inside a particular religious culture whose self-confidence and self-importance had not, before 1914, been compelled to come to terms with external criticism.

As an individual, Temple did not find it difficult to tolerate the unquestioningly religious education that he was given as a child. He was the kind of parson's son who cannot reject his father's beliefs. This willingness to accept a Christian outlook was complicated by a kind of innocence about how difficult it might be to apply Christianity to society. He had no doubts about religion as such: he was sure that one could trust the underlying rationality of the world in which one lived, that in the last analysis the universe made sense. As a result his intellectual willingness to feel that evil played a necessary part in the theological description of human life was balanced by a persistent belief that at the political level a wide range of human suffering was preventable and therefore ought to be prevented. This is always a difficult position for a Christian thinker to sustain, because Christian tradition, steeped in the idea that there is a fundamental spiritual value to be found in suffering, is against him, and because powerful forms of conservative political thought have, especially since the French Revolution, constantly used the pessimistic side of Christian doctrine to argue that suffering is inevitable. Throughout his career Temple balanced orthodox-looking statements about the part which suffering plays in the Christian description of human redemption with demands for radical political change.

One reason for this was that as a young man his Christian outlook had been penetrated by a mood of social anxiety which was widely prevalent in the Victorian upper class from which he came. After a precocious intellectual start at Rugby, a school at which his father had been headmaster from 1857 to 1869 and which was still being run on consciously liberal Anglican lines in the 1890s, he went to Balliol College, Oxford, in 1900. This meant that his original clerical formation, for one is bound to call it that, was exposed to a wider more secular mood of doubt about the health of British society. This doubt had its sources in the rapid growth of industrial England in the nineteenth century and went on affecting British politics decisively until after the Second World War. The social self-criticism which had begun to penetrate Oxford in the 1880s especially in the shape of the Hegelian philosophy and Liberal politics of T. H. Green sprang from the conviction that the economic and imperial successes of Victorian individualism had made too many comfortably-off people indifferent to the effects of industrialisation on society. The ensuing debate was not, like the more recent debate in Britain which followed realisation of the longterm national consequences of the Second World War, about national failure, but a debate about what should be done with apparent national success, both at home and in the

Empire. Politically, this reaction helped to produce the Labour Party and meant that some members of the Liberal Party, the New Liberals, made a short-lived break with that party's suspicion of state action. Neither of these political groups owed much to religious forces.

Awareness that fresh conflict was developing between the economically powerful and the economically dependent had therefore unsettled a group of Anglicans in the generation before Temple's. The most important were the High Churchmen gathered round Scott Holland and Charles Gore in the Christian Social Union which they helped to found in 1889. The Union's basic aim, which was 'to claim for Christian law the ultimate authority to rule social practice', wildly exceeded any practical influence which the British churches could exercise on economic behaviour, but many in the Anglican sub-culture did not recognise this weakness. Temple joined the CSU while he was at Oxford and remained active in it for some years, but could never bend it to a useful purpose.

The effect of the social excitements of the time on Temple as a student can be seen in a letter written in 1901 in which he spoke of the need

to identify religion with life. For this, intellect is needed – and of course spirit too: it is not that we now need a different and a lower faculty – but that we need the old spiritual zeal with intellect to direct it. And apart from the greatness of such a work itself, if it can be done the Housing Problem, the Temperance Question, the differences between employer and employed will solve themselves, and the British Empire will become an instrument of real justice (not just legal codes) and real education – not the doctrine of practical success. (Iremonger, 1948, p. 100)

Temple's career in Oxford lasted for ten years. He became a Fellow of Queen's College in 1904 and lectured on Plato's *Republic* and philosophical topics like 'the nature of personality'. He was ordained to the Anglican ministry in 1909; and the resemblance to his father's career was strengthened when in 1910 he became Headmaster of Repton. In his pursuit of ordination, however, he had a set-back, because when he approached Paget, the Bishop of Oxford, in 1906, Paget refused to ordain him on the ground that he was prepared to assent only tentatively to what Paget regarded as the orthodox understanding of the Virgin Birth and the Bodily Resurrection of Jesus as being both historical and supernatural events.

Temple's driving-force at that moment was the conviction that he had a mission to reform the Church of England. This was not surprising in itself: when a young man of considerable intellectual ability like Temple finds himself drawn to organised religion, he is likely to discover that organised religion needs to be reformed. Doctrinal changes, however, were not high on his list. He always preferred to allow theological opinions to find their own level in free discussion, and he seems to have expected Anglican bishops to take the same line. Paget's refusal to ordain him on his own terms was the twenty-five-year old's first real experience of the intensity of Anglican theological divisions, a problem to which he never found a satisfactory answer.

In episcopal churches, when a bishop refuses one ordination, it is common practice to approach another. Temple acted cautiously, but in 1908 he asked Randall Davidson, the Archbishop of Canterbury and an old friend of his father, for an interview, as a result of which the Archbishop negotiated with Paget, who did not completely withdraw his own objection, but accepted Davidson's offer to ordain Temple himself at Canterbury. Davidson was not going to lose Temple's undoubted promise for the sake of what he called 'undergraduate' arguments, and told Paget that he regarded Temple 'as being *in all essential particulars*, an orthodox believer in the Virgin Birth of Our Blessed Lord and in His

Resurrection. I do not say that he expresses himself respecting either truth with the distinctness (at least as to detail) which has been usual in Orthodox Theology. But I can see no adequate reason why he should not be now ordained' (Iremonger, 1948, p. 116).

How far Davidson understood Temple's theological position it is hard to say; perhaps he did not want to know too exactly how the young radical defined his terms.

The other major event of Temple's Oxford career had been his falling under the sway of the idealist philosophy of the Master of Balliol, Edward Caird, who after T. H. Green's death in 1882 had become the leading Hegelian thinker in Oxford. The result, which may well have influenced Davidson, was a series of addresses given by Temple to students in November–December 1909 and published, with the title The Faith and Modern Thought, in 1910. Many of Temple's later positions can already be found here.

Temple set out to give a coherent view of the relationship between Christianity and philosophy, and he did so by taking as central to our understanding of the universe the idea of Purpose. He argued that such a universal Purpose could not exist without the active presence of a real Will which lay 'behind' the world. Purposeful action, moreover, must (or so it seemed to Temple) be personal, and this in turn suggested that the 'creative purpose' behind the world must also be Personal. In this way Temple built up the idea of a 'Governing Will', or personal 'god'.

Temple then answered the problem of 'the faith and modern thought' by asserting that what one encountered in one's own religious experience (and he meant Christian experience, though he did not always say so) was this personal Purpose at the heart of the universe. Switching from speculation to Christian theology he identified this supranatural personality with the God described in the New

Testament in terms of Jesus Christ, who (orthodox tradition claimed) had been the objective, historical and once-for-all self-revelation of the divine in human form. Aware that the greatest objection to his argument that the universe made sense in terms of a divine Purpose was the undeniable presence of evil in the resulting system, he described Jesus as the solution to the problem of evil because he enabled the believer to overcome evil in himself. Temple claimed that when one contemplated the Crucifixion of Jesus, one had to admit one's individual impotence to change oneself for the better; instead, one was changed as one contemplated the Crucifixion.

Temple summed up his concept of God in terms of an optimistic account of human history down to 1910:

remembering that the world has progressed a good deal since the earliest ages that we know, and progressed in love more perhaps than in any other quality, we shall find that it may be true that the whole world is moving forwards for ever under the impulse of the infinite love of God to a more and more adequate return of that love; we begin to think of the whole universe as knit together in that love as its one controlling principle. (Temple, 1910, pp. 136–7)

By 1910 it was clear that Temple's life was to be public rather than private, ecclesiastical rather than philosophical, and political rather than pietist. He devoted most of the summer of 1910 to the Student Christian Movement, then in its brief heyday as the ecumenical think-tank of the Protestant churches. His political impulses had already been significantly stirred when he chaired an SCM Conference on 'Christianity and Social Problems' at Matlock in 1909. He now spent six weeks visiting Australian universities as a spokesman for the Movement, which also sent him as a steward to the Edinburgh World Missionary Conference. The Edinburgh Conference is regularly described as the start of

the twentieth-century ecumenical movement, which culminated for Temple in 1938 when he became provisional
chairman of the self-styled World Council of Churches, the
formal inauguration of which was delayed until after his
death by the Second World War. The Edinburgh Conference
also marked the high point of Victorian missionary confidence that Christianity could replace the religious cultures of
countries like India and China. Western religious influence in
the East crumbled steadily after 1914, but Temple's belief that
history was on the side of an expanding Christianity never left
him. This explains the phenomenal energy which he put into
constructing the network of personal contacts and international committees which finally produced the World
Council of Churches.

By 1910, released by ordination from uncertainty about his
future, Temple's desire to act on the public stage was already
very strong, but his move from Oxford to become Headmaster of Repton School gave him little useful experience. He
rationalised his decision to go there by letting it be known
that he thought that the public schools reproduced and even
accentuated British class-divisions and that he hoped to
change the situation, but for once in his life Temple found it
impossible to create any kind of movement. As long as he
stayed at Repton, he was obliged to play the role of clerical
public-school headmaster who also taught Classics. What he
wanted, and by this time knew that he wanted, was room to
assert himself in Anglican politics, and by the end of 1912 he
would have left Repton for St Margaret's, Westminster but
for a legal technicality. As it was, he had to wait until May
1914 when he escaped to the fashionable London church of St
James's, Piccadilly.

Temple's lack of success at Repton did not affect his
development. He was deeply influenced by the views of R. H.
Tawney, a fellow Anglican and professional historian who

became a prominent figure in the Labour Party. They had known each other since they were both at Rugby. Temple conducted Tawney's marriage ceremony in 1909, and Tawney dedicated his first important book, The Agrarian Problem of the Sixteenth Century (1912), to Temple and Albert Mansbridge, the principal founder of the Workers' Educational Association in 1903.

Tawney was a High Anglican Christian socialist who dismissed as unrealistic 'the dualism which draws a sharp line between the life of the spirit, which is the sphere of religion, and the external order with which religion has no concern'. The church should not take its economic and social views from one class or party, as had happened too often in the past, but should state its own conception of the duties and rights of people in society, and decide its attitude to political parties by that standard (Tawney, 1953, p. 177, from a paper written for the 1937 Oxford Conference on Church, Community and State). This was the strategy which Temple advocated for Anglicanism, though Adrian Hastings, for whom Tawney was close to being the Thomas More of the twentieth century, thought that Temple did not really share Tawney's preoccupation with equality as a guiding social aim. This was true in the sense that Temple, for example, accepted episcopal membership of the House of Lords, whereas Tawney drily turned down the offer of a peerage, but the social programmes which Temple put together always had greater equality – in housing, health provision, education and so on – as their consequence. Tawney did not share Temple's optimism about changing the Church of England and devoted his political energy to the secular Labour Party, over which he had considerable intellectual influence between the World Wars.

It was Tawney who had persuaded Temple to attend the first national conference of the WEA in Oxford in 1905.

Temple recognised that the WEA was not only an experiment in adult education, but also an effort to cross the division between upper- and working-class schools; he taught for it, as Tawney did, from 1907 to 1914, and he was President of the Association from 1908 until 1924. In 1915, in *Church and Nation*, he praised the Association's university tutorial classes because they sought to combine the spirit of traditional education (or of Oxford, as the text implies) with the greater energy and efficiency of the modern. In practice, the WEA was formed too late to have much political or educational importance, but for Temple and Tawney it expressed an evangelistic desire to get at and alter the moral attitudes of the new industrial society. 'There is no limit to the range of the influence of education', Temple wrote in *Church and Nation*: 'it is the supreme regenerative force' (p. 193). Both men thought that educational reform was the key to preventing the sharper social conflict which so many Edwardians dreaded, and Temple, provided 'education' was understood as fundamentally 'religious education', never changed his views. In his last major statement on social questions, *Christianity and Social Order* (1942), he declared that

there is one great division in our educational scheme. The so-called Public Schools, which have held the corporate tradition strongly throughout their long history, have been inaccessible to the poorer children. This was probably inevitable in a period when education as a whole had become a perquisite of the wealthier section of society. It is on the way to being a shocking anomaly as education is made available to the whole community. That what is generally thought to be the best form of education should be reserved to those whose parents are able to pay expensive fees, or expensive preparatory school education with a view to the winning of scholarships, makes a cleavage in the educational and social life of the country as a whole, which is destructive of the best fellowship. (p. 91)

Nevertheless, his experiences at Repton persuaded him that a school could express the Spirit of Christ and so the kind of world in which people ought to live. This explains the romantic statement in his farewell Repton sermon that 'selfishness and even self-centredness unfits a boy, in proportion to its intensity, for effective membership of his House or School' (Temple, 1914a, p. 232). Neither before nor after the Great War did he think of the religious side of the schools as helping to make inequality respectable. Nor was he entirely committed to the common Edwardian vision of the public schools as the source of a stream of gentlemanly Christian bureaucrats and colonial officials, deeply opposed to materialism but sound on a Christian empire. He spoke in the same Repton sermon of a renunciation of the world – 'the World which is, roughly speaking, represented by the *Times* and the *Spectator*' – a definition which, taken seriously, would have pointed his sixth-form hearers to the fringe rather than the centre of the society outside their school. There were moments when the preacher's language, if not the preacher himself, was demanding that his hearers anticipate in their own actions a drastic reformation of the economic structure of British society. He talked at times as though the public schools were 'mission schools' dedicated to forming a Christian elite in a foreign land.

So far we have considered the way in which Temple's career developed his ideas in terms of theology, ecumenism and education. While he was still at Repton he published *The Kingdom of God* (1914a; the lectures were given in 1912), the best evidence for his early social ideas. It was based on talks which he had given to Cambridge students earlier in 1912. The underlying creative emotion was already firmly established. 'No one', he said, 'is content with the present social condition of England' (p. 74). There was an unjustifiable gap in Britain between a considerable number of comparatively wealthy people and another large group which suffered from want and destitution. 'If you take some millions of people just like ourselves, generous up to a point but still predominantly selfish, with varying abilities, and leave them to live together for several generations, the result will be something like the horror of our present European civilisation' (p. 75). He asserted that 'our home society is in ruins . . . it actually is a mass of rivalries and hostilities, capital against labour and labour against capital, firm against firm, man against man' (p. 78). The framework of the Christian society which ought to replace it would have to be 'socialistic'. 'Whether this will take the form of direct state ownership, or of state control of privately owned capital' was largely indifferent, 'but the community will not allow that any great occupation of men [i.e. a major industry] can be something indifferent to it, which it can leave to run its own course' (p. 79). The 'Christian state' would be a community which took responsibility for the spiritual and economic welfare of each individual, while expecting each individual to recognise his own responsibility to the whole community.

What Temple wrote did not spell out a political programme but a state of mind. 'Competition', he alleged, 'is not a thing limited to business; it is a thing that pervades our whole life. It is simply organised selfishness . . . A great deal has been said in praise of competition and most of it is rubbish . . . It is sometimes said that if you want to get the best out of a man you must appeal to his own interest. That brings us to the crucial point. For if that is true Christ was wrong. The whole gospel rests upon the presupposition of the denial of that statement' (pp. 96–8). Temple was reflecting the feelings of a part of the middle classes which was not directly involved in the conflicts between employers and employed, which was more and more horrified by the spectacle, and which found in its religious sentiments support for its distress at social conflict.

When Temple turned from the economic policy of the Christian state to the way in which it would treat its criminals, he deliberately contrasted Edwardian penal practice with a utopian Christian vision. For criminals there would be neither retributive, nor deterrent, nor even reformative punishment, but the offender's heart and will would be changed by the readiness of his victim to suffer at his hands (p. 80). This was appealing directly to what Matthew Arnold called the method of Jesus, but the real force of this optimistic statement sprang from the well-documented failure of the Victorian prison system, which had been based on theories of reformative punishment. Temple was saying something very like what Elizabeth Fry had said once she had grasped the nature of the early Victorian penitentiary, that such imprisonment, even when flavoured with sermons, was anti-Christian by nature.

Temple took the same line when he turned to the question of poverty. The Edwardian answer was still essentially 'charity', but to be Christian, Temple argued, charity would have to be indiscriminate and impartial, an assertion which directly contradicted the popular ethos of the Charity Organisation Society, a voluntary body, which ensured as far as possible that charity was given only to the 'deserving' poor after they had survived a vigorous testing of 'character'. A century of disagreement about the proper attitude to poverty was latent in Temple's words, and his views were closer to the ethos of the Welfare State of the 1960s than they were to the practice of the Victorian churches.

Finally, in the case of international affairs, Temple stated that a Christian nation would be prepared to defend others who were being oppressed, but that, as far as its own interests were concerned, it would prefer its own disappearance to the stain of the passion of war (p. 83). It is interesting that even when he was putting forward a deliberately provocative interpretation of the New Testament, Temple made no real concession to pacifism. A sacrificial war for the sake of others was permissible, and this was to become the typical Anglican justification of the war which broke out in 1914. Temple never moved in a pacifist direction, and he already took the ground, which he firmly defended in the 1930s against a powerful Anglican pacifist movement led by H. R. L. Sheppard and Charles Raven, that the Christian citizen of a state which was not itself Christian should not refuse to fight for abstract theological reasons, 'because if he does he may be putting himself entirely out of touch with the great stream of life which at the moment may be a far nobler thing than any practicable alternative' (Temple, 1914a, p. 91).

One catches a foretaste of the exultation which ran round Europe as the Great War began, but Temple meant more than that. His political philosophy was Greek as well as Christian and turned on the classical idea that the good life of the individual can only be lived as part of a community. The individual could only fulfil himself as a human being in a society which trained and equipped him to do so; he was not autonomous, he could not contract out, nor could he invent his own social existence and so escape the consequences of living in a sick society. Conversely, the troubles of a sick society could only be cured by remedies applied to the society as a whole. One might call this the 'liberal' side of Temple's Anglicanism, because he always assumed that the community would use its power to increase the freedom of the individual; he was not satisfied with the orthodox view that all that religion could do was save individuals from an incurably sick society.

In spite of this, it would be wrong to suppose that in the years before 1914 political theology was a major issue for

young Anglican intellectuals. The mainstream churches had
entered the twentieth century still entangled in longstanding
Victorian anxieties about the credibility of the miracle stories
of the New Testament and about the status of the founder of
Christianity: was he only human, or was he both human and
divine? The question had confused Temple's plans for
ordination, and the wider controversy was brought to a head
in 1911 when a radical Oxford Dean of Divinity, J. M.
Thompson, published a book called *Miracles in the New Testament*
in which he rejected all the New Testament miracle stories
and with them the traditional doctrine of the divinity of
Christ. Part of the reply to Thompson was *Foundations: A
Statement of Christian Belief in Terms of Modern Thought*, by Seven
Oxford Men (1912).

For all the apparently liberal intentions of *Foundations*, to
which Thompson was not asked to contribute, Temple's own
essay, on 'The Divinity of Christ' (pp. 211–64), seems
orthodox – Christ was both God and Man. Before his
ordination, Temple had hesitated at crudely historical
descriptions of the Virgin Birth and the Resurrection of
Christ. Now he ignored the problem of history and instead
applied his favourite philosophical terminology of will and
purpose. Christ's will was at one with his Father's and our
human purposes had to become Christ's purpose in order to
be fully human. He swept Thompson's reasonable doubts
about the New Testament miracle stories aside with the
assertion that 'if a man is thus [like Christ] united to God,
Nature is his servant, not his master, and he may (so the story
tells us) walk upon the water' (Streeter, 1912, p. 259).
Walking on water did not really matter to Temple, because
that was 'history'; what did matter was the risen Christ's
capacity to change a person's will and purpose not in New
Testament narratives but in Edwardian England. Temple's
theological intention was to keep open a path to orthodox

conclusions, protecting orthodoxy against the liberal passion for doctrinal redefinition.

When the Great War began in 1914, Temple was recently established in London at St James's, Piccadilly. His mother died in 1915, and he married Frances Anson in 1916. From then until 1926 his career advanced steadily. This was partly because the outbreak of war itself had no devastating emotional effect on him. He had no doubt that Britain had been morally bound to declare war in August 1914, and was no less bound to carry the war to a decisive end. In 1915 he said that the war was being fought 'to determine whether in the next period the Christian or the directly anti-Christian method shall have an increase of influence' (Temple, 1915, p. xii). Yet he was never a clerical recruiting sergeant in the style of the Bishop of London, Winnington-Ingram. The only emotional satisfaction that he could find in the war was that it might present the opportunity for positive change in church and society. As a clergyman he could not share the fighting soldier's experience, and he never felt, as his friend Tawney did by 1917, that the war was being fought largely from inertia, as an end in itself. He trusted the official view of the war even after the first battle of the Somme in 1916, because theologically he wanted to believe that the massive butchery which he was reading about made some sense in the mind of God. The orthodox side of his personality pushed him at first to the conclusion that the national religious response to the war should be collective repentance, an act which, if it had taken place would have transferred the responsibility for events from God and worldly governments to people in general. This was the spur of the National Mission of Repentance and Hope, in which he took a full part.

The more objective religious implications of what was happening reached him through anxious Army chaplains who reported that Christianity played little part in the life of the vast majority of soldiers, that the alleged Victorian revival of Christianity, whether Evangelical or Anglo-Catholic, had been confined to limited middle-class religious groups and that the Church of England itself needed drastic institutional reform to make it less clerical, less hierarchical and less remote. In England it seemed equally clear as the war proceeded that the existing relationship between the two sides of industry could not remain unchanged, and Temple, who briefly joined the Labour Party in 1918, withdrawing when he became Bishop of Manchester in 1921, took for granted that if the English church was to justify its establishment by providing the bonding sentiment of British society, it must take a positive part in any discussion of social reconstruction.

The result was a complicated pattern of activity which we shall discuss in more detail in later chapters. He wrote incessantly: apart from other commitments he edited a centre-party Anglican weekly newspaper, *Challenge*, from 1915 until 1918, producing leader after leader on the changing war situation. He found time to complete *Mens Creatrix* (1917), his first full-scale theological work, which combined an account of his philosophical theology with a broad impression of the social thought which he linked to it. In 1916 he became one of the secretaries of the unsuccessful National Mission of Repentance and Hope. In the same year he joined the Archbishops' Committee on Church and State, of which he was the youngest member at thirty-five. Once the report, which recommended greater self-government for the established church, was issued, he became intensely anxious that reforming the Church of England should begin even before the war ended, and in July 1917 he presided over the meeting at the Queen's Hall in London which inaugurated the Life and Liberty Movement, a pressure-group which briefly looked like an internal Anglican insurrection.

He had at last found an outlet for the ideas which the war was stirring in him, and he resigned as rector of St James's, Piccadilly so that he could organise Life and Liberty full time. For a moment Temple and his friends seemed to be threatening to switch to disestablishment if they were denied the changes they wanted, but the crisis passed quickly. The Enabling Act of 1919 set up a National Assembly (always called the Church Assembly) which had three Houses (Bishops, Clergy and Laity) and which could propose a limited variety of measures to Parliament which became law if not challenged within thirty days. There was no risk of internal democracy, because the Bishops had final control; externally, Parliament had still the power to reject whatever the Assembly proposed.

Although Temple published his second important theological work, *Christus Veritas*, in 1924, first and foremost he was now an Anglican politician who thought that the established church had a natural political role to play in English society which it could only play properly if it had a liberalised constitution which gave more power to the laity, an internal agreement to differ on disputed theological questions and a social theology which rejected Victorian individualism. These positions were concrete, they did not depend on a theory of 'progress', and they were Temple's serious attempt to persuade, not just Anglicanism, but the whole Christian sub-culture, which he ardently desired to unite, to do more than passively reflect the deep divisions, made more visible by the war, which plagued (and still plague) English society. When Temple said in 1918 that the world was 'plastic', he was making the point, which contemporary secular politicians also recognised, that the war, by its scale, its savagery, its internal effects on the countries which had fought it, had created a brief moment of flux of which Temple, as a politician, strove to take advantage while it lasted.

Unfortunately, the new, partially representative Church Assembly reflected only too faithfully the patterns of disagreement in Anglicanism which made further change indecisive and slow in coming. It is characteristic of churches that they may have a common statement of belief, but they rarely if ever have a common theology. This applies equally in the area of political theology, where Temple did not create the consensus which he hoped would follow from the reports which came from the interdenominational Conference on Politics, Economics and Citizenship (hereafter 'Copec'), which he organised in Birmingham in 1924. Temple's views never dominated the Church Assembly, and once he had been identified as 'socialist', he was steadily and sometimes very bitterly attacked by other Anglican public figures, like Hensley Henson, the Bishop of Durham (1920–39), who denounced him for political intervention while himself intervening frequently on the Conservative side.

By 1926, moreover, the momentum for change which had developed in the later stages of the war was exhausted, and a sign of a new era was the General Strike in May 1926. On the one hand there was a half-hearted, defensive, almost suicidal cry for social protection from the trade unions, who had been alarmed at the treatment of the miners by the mine-owners, and on the other there was the over-elated middle-class organisation of force in defence of what was felt to be a threatened social order. The strike was called off after nine days, during which the Baldwin government claimed that a general strike was illegal; there followed a long drawn-out struggle between the mine-owners and the miners, which ended in the miners' total defeat.

The General Strike cruelly exposed the gap between ecclesiastical conferences and industrial conflict, and underlined the fact, of which Temple was aware, that there was no Anglican party among the miners. Copec had been designed to strengthen a current of middle-class opinion and in the longer run no doubt did so: it is not fanciful to identify Copec's ideas as one source of the support which surrounded the Welfare State in the 1950s. But Copec's primary target was the religious sub-culture itself: there was no question of forming a political group in the style of the Catholic political parties on the Continent; there was not even a strong Copec association to play a direct part in the crisis of 1926. In a late Victorian tradition which assumed that in all industrial conflict there was a common interest between employers and employed, and that reconciliation was the essential Christian contribution to such situations, the Archbishop of Canterbury tried to mediate, but the government, which did not want the situation moralised, effectively silenced him.

Temple himself was unwell and abroad in May 1926. When he returned and saw the miners' strike still continuing, he joined a further unsuccessful effort at mediation in July 1926. This had been launched by an unofficial inter-denominational group which included several Anglican bishops. This intervention has often been criticised on the ground that it was unrealistic, but it was less a refusal to face the reality of power than a reasonable protest in Christian terms against the way in which power was being used. Realism is not always a matter of recognising and choosing the winning side.

Nevertheless, 1926 marked the end of any hopes which Temple might have had that the Life and Liberty campaign, the setting-up of the Church Assembly and the focusing of religious attention on social problems which had been achieved at Birmingham in 1924 would release new reforming energy in the Church of England to help it to justify its survival as a state church. Throughout the 1920s the unfinished Victorian conflict between Evangelicals and Anglo-Catholics absorbed what energy was available, and when the Church Assembly finally put forward to Parliament a compromise revision of the Anglican Prayer Book, the House of Commons rejected it in 1927/8. There followed a barren controversy about 'church establishment'.

Temple himself was not excited by the controversies which divided Evangelical and Anglo-Catholic, and still less by the enthusiasm for disestablishment which flared up briefly in Anglican circles as a response to the action of Parliament. By the time that hostilities were dying away the world slump which followed the Stock Market Crash of 1929 had brought down the MacDonald Labour government in 1931 and put the Conservatives in power for the rest of the decade. The New Liberalism, which was perhaps a more natural political home for Temple than the Labour Party, had disintegrated with the Liberal Party. A siege mentality developed in all the churches as they became aware that economic and intellectual difficulties were increasing together, that their membership was falling and that their ethical judgements no longer counted for much in the wider society. There was no foreseeable future for left-of-centre Anglican social theology in this political environment, which was rapidly dominated by the problems of unemployment and foreign policy. Temple was enthroned as Archbishop of York in January 1929, and so became ever more deeply involved in the day-to-day running of the still cumbersome Anglican machine. Nevertheless, between 1932 and 1934 he gave the Gifford Lectures on natural theology which were published in 1934 as *Nature, Man and God*, his third major exercise in theological reconstruction.

The one cause with which Temple was identified which quickly caught the imagination of influential groups in Anglicanism was ecumenism, the movement to unite the separated Christian churches. It gathered considerable momentum in the inter-war period. Unfortunately, the movement was easily tempted to become another forum for disputes about the nature of the masculine priesthood, related to those which were dividing Anglicanism in the same period. Between 1926 and his death in 1944 Temple became the undisputed world leader and major statesman of the ecumenical movement. He played a fundamental part in setting up the structure of the self-styled World Council of Churches (the Roman Catholic Church did not join the Council), which was formally inaugurated in Amsterdam in 1948, four years after he died. He realised that if national churches everywhere were losing their role in contemporary culture – and here the situation had worsened in the 1930s as Stalinism, which was consciously materialist, tightened its grip on Russia, while Nazism and Fascism tried to make the cult of the nation-state into a totalitarian substitute for traditional religion – part of their salvation could lie in uniting at least world Protestantism. There was more doubt than he had originally thought about the resources which Protestantism actually had. By the 1960s the World Council had lost hope of any early unification of the mainstream Protestant churches, while the growing interest of the Vatican in ecumenical affairs limited Protestant freedom of action.

How highly should one rate what Temple achieved in his work for the ecumenical movement? Adrian Hastings has no doubt of the World Council's importance in the 1930s:

The ecumenical movement had grown with the League of Nations and must have seemed at times in the comfortable twenties but a pale religious reflection of the League's secular aspirations. But now the League was breaking down, its aspirations scorned. Faced with the challenge of Nazism and stiffened by the revival of a more conservative theology the churches of the thirties and still more the ecumenical movement of the thirties saw themselves as the Church over against the world . . . The ecumenical movement and its earlier international organisations long claimed to be in no way a replacement for existing churches. In a profound way, however, in the thirties the movement felt called to make of itself a unified body precisely so as to fulfil the first duty of the Church and witness in faith and with independence to the world of sin, modern ideology, and secular tyranny when the [independent national] Churches could, or would, not do it. (Hastings, 1986, p. 305)

This verdict exaggerates the importance of the World Council's protests against 'modern ideology and secular tyranny', which were not always as united as Hastings implies, and were no more effective than those of the Vatican. The Council was still only shakily put together and was much more an alliance of individuals than a federation of churches. Nevertheless, Temple deserved much credit for the fact that this new world Christian body was there at all.

An additional reason for Temple's preoccupation with ecumenical affairs in the 1930s was that Cosmo Lang followed Davidson as Archbishop of Canterbury from 1928 to 1942. Lang was already sixty-four when he took office and had nothing new to say to the Church of England. He was often unwell, and Temple, now Archbishop of York, had to stand in for him from time to time. Lang agreed with Baldwin that Edward VIII should abdicate in 1936, enjoyed the coronation of George VI, which he regarded as the climax of his ecclesiastical life, and campaigned reproachfully and unsuccessfully for a 'Recall to Religion' in 1937. There was no question of looking to the future: the scheme for Prayer Book revision which foundered in 1927/8 had been Davidson and Lang's last serious effort to modernise the Anglican Church, if the Prayer Book changes deserved that description.

Temple did his best from York, but this was an apprehensive, under-organised decade in England, dominated by too many men whose fundamental experience was a debilitating mixture of Edwardianism and the Great War. Temple had suffered less than most from the war, and he fiercely resisted the wave of religious pacifism which passed over the British churches in the mid thirties. Even so, when the Second World War began in 1939, he startled many people by saying at intervals that war had to have reasonable aims, and that to demand unconditional surrender was bad diplomacy.

Already, before he was promoted to Lambeth in 1942, he was trying to put together a new movement for social reform, guessing rightly that those who had governed England between the wars would have to pay a domestic price for victory in Europe. The Malvern Conference, which set out the Archbishop's social agenda, was held as early as January 1941. *Christianity and Social Order*, a paperback written specially for Penguin, appeared in 1942 but had been finished by November 1941. It was the most popular of his books, selling 140,000 copies. Once again he made his case for a Christian politics which aimed at increasing social equality rather than accepting inequality and then mounting a Christian ambulance service whose charity could never help more than a minority of the underprivileged. Perhaps he was soft on fact and strong on sentiment, as some have said; perhaps he had still not entirely learned the theological lesson of social pessimism which his orthodox critics ardently desire to teach him even now. But his crisp assertion, as the head of the state church, that in various fields – health, housing, employment, education, for example – ordinary people deserved better of the English social system than they were receiving carried its own conviction in many quarters. Twice in the first half of the century ordinary people had been expected to fight to defend what they and others had, but few had asked them whether they thought that what they had was worth defending. It is not surprising that after 1945 there should have been a British Welfare State, and William Temple was one of those who contributed much to its foundations.

# Chapter 2

# Modernising the church

The idea of modernising the Church of England had attracted people throughout the nineteenth century, but for most of them church reform meant little more than doing away with 'abuses', with the way in which the eighteenth-century ruling classes had subordinated the Establishment to its own interests. The abolition of 'abuses', of the sale of livings, for example, fitted into the popular early Victorian political idea of increased efficiency, and answered a rising demand that the state church should justify its privileges. Temple's idea of modernisation was much wider than this and much less obsessed with the controversy about disestablishing the Church of England: he dreamed of reidentifying church and nation, and of making the Anglican Church in its turn the centre of a worldwide Christian unity.

By the end of the nineteenth century the Nonconformist campaign against the Establishment was fading, though this was a failure of Nonconformity rather than a victory for the reformers of the state church. Inside the Church of England itself, the Anglo-Catholic party which had formed in the 1830s had often deplored the state's power over the church but had never seriously demanded disestablishment. Anglican Evangelicals, whose sense of a separate identity went back into the eighteenth century, had actually defended the status quo because they feared that the new and apparently expanding Anglo-Catholic group would dominate an Anglicanism freed from parliamentary control. As for English Roman Catholicism, on the one hand, the Vatican's denial of the validity of Anglican priestly orders in 1896 had committed English Catholics to a hostile critique of the Church of England, but on the other hand the Vatican-inspired persecution of George Tyrrell and the Catholic Modernists after 1907 did not suggest that English Catholics were free in some sense that Anglicans were not. In Temple's Edwardian youth there was no obvious threat to establishment other than the increasing secularity of English society, which made a state church seem out of date, especially one which took up inordinate amounts of valuable parliamentary time. It was this quiet, persistent and growing secular criticism which prompted Anglican interest in change from the 1880s and led to the formation of the Church Reform League in 1896.

There were three broad grounds to be made for preserving the Church of England. The broadest ground of all was that the church was already there, an immense social institution still closely integrated into English society at many points, so that in the Edwardian period disestablishment proper would have entailed much greater social confusion than had attended the disestablishment of the Irish church in the 1860s, or would attend similar action in Wales after the First World War. There was a set of cultural references here as well: to the monarchy, to the older universities and public schools, to the cathedrals; to the Authorised Version and the Book of Common Prayer in their still unamended forms; to a distinct tradition of religious poetry; to an arcadian (but also political) England of squire and parson. Disestablishment, it could be argued, would make sense only as the ultimate expression of a much wider cultural revolution. Temple accepted this view of Anglicanism, and could write quite seriously in 1928 that 'whether logical or not, the English method has always been to enjoy all kinds of excellence together as far as possible, retaining the glamour and unifying influence of monarchy with the steadying influence of hereditary aristocracy while welcoming the progressive impetus of democracy . . . The Church of England, like other Churches, has often failed to be completely christian – always, indeed, if we take those words in all their proper depth of meaning; but it has never failed to be utterly, completely, provokingly, adorably English' (in Temple, 1958, pp. 88–90).

The second ground, which was religious, and which did not require establishment as such, was the assertion that all other churches, including the Church of Rome, represented Christian extremes, but that Anglicanism was a fusion of extremes, combining what was best in both Protestantism and Catholicism. 'The Church of England', Temple wrote, 'sought to combine the strong elements of both traditions; it has held them in rather unstable equilibrium; they have until lately rather existed side by side than coalesced into a real unity' (Temple, 1958, p. 91). That these religious extremes coalesced in Anglicanism was exposed as an exaggeration in 1928, when the quarrel over the Prayer Book between Evangelical and Anglo-Catholic came to a head, but they did coexist. Looked at in this way, the Church of England was not simply to be defined in terms of its sixteenth-century origins and then dismissed as an out-moded example of Protestant Christianity, in the familiar Roman Catholic manner, but could be interpreted as showing a line of true development from the apostolic past which other churches would do well to follow. This conception of Anglican development had grown up in the nineteenth century as an answer to the internal conflict which had arisen between Anglican Evangelicals, Liberals and Anglo-Catholics, and was sounder than

Newman's inherently conservative doctrine of Catholic development, which was forced on him by his need to give logical coherence to the history of Vatican theology.

The third, political, ground was the argument that ideally the state church should not only express the religion of the English people but should also bond them together as a political nation in the acceptance of common attitudes to life. To non-Anglicans in 1900 this theory looked like a survival from late seventeenth-century High Church theory, in which, as G. V. Bennett said, 'the Church of England . . . received from the civil power continual support and comfort in its role as the guardian of the morals and religious duties of the nation . . . in return the Church fostered loyalty and obedience with all the ideological resources at its command, in the education of the young, in the elaboration of social and political theory, and by its influence as a major landowner' (Bennett, 1975, p. 295). The church's social and educational work had not freed it from the state's constitutional control over episcopal appointments and over the arrangements for worship and discipline. Early twentieth-century Roman Catholics and Nonconformists found in their own existence proof that English society had lost the homogeneity which might once have justified the theory. Their views, however, were less important than the Victorian growth of a new industrial society in which the majority of the urban working classes belonged neither to the Establishment nor to its religious critics. Fear of social conflict rose sharply in the late nineteenth century, and this helps to explain why some late Victorian bishops and public-school headmasters offered an up-to-date version of the 'Church and King' tradition in the form of a spiritualised cult of empire. One has constantly to remind oneself that Temple was a product of this period, 1880–1914, when England seemed to itself, despite the emotional shock of the South African War, to be unique among nations, the dominant world power, with an apparently unlimited future.

By the end of the nineteenth century the Church of England was reasserting itself as the national church. Many Anglicans, Temple among them, were not impressed by claims that establishment was no longer religiously justifiable. While they admitted that the Establishment might have lost contact with the mass of the people, as was to be fully confirmed by Army chaplain experience during the First World War, they maintained that the state church could justify its existence in the twentieth century by changing that situation. There was a reversion to the vision of a close partnership between church and state in which religious and moral education would be the church's most important contribution. This was what Temple had in mind, for example, when as late as 1942 he said that schools must foster both individual development and world fellowship; they must encourage individualism but also create bonds of union with fellow citizens and citizens of other nations. 'There is only one candidate for this double function', he said; 'it is Christianity. We must then take steps to secure that the corporate life of the schools is Christian' (Temple, 1942, p. 92).

Temple responded to the problems of the Church of England's future by means of an elaborate programme of reform. He set out a theological system which would support his overall social aim of a redeemed, organic, national community expressing itself religiously through the Church of England. This implied the expansion of religious education, ideally so that all education would take place in a 'religious' context: as in Newman's case, unreformed, Anglican-dominated Oxford still haunted the educational imagination. In addition, the constitution of the Church of England had to be changed to make the establishment more rational, more efficient, and more democratic, above all by allowing the laity to share in the government of the church, both locally and through some kind of central assembly. In Temple's mind, at any rate during the wartime campaign to set up the Church Assembly, this would make more effective political intervention possible. This he regarded as a proper consequence of the church's mere existence; he was anxious to add to the episcopal politics of influence at Westminster a politics of public pressure, even of the church as a deliberate pressure-group, a policy which would bear some fruit after the conferences at Birmingham in 1924 and at Malvern in 1941. Finally, he wanted to move beyond the national to an international framework: he was one of a small group of Christian leaders who saw a united world church as a powerful instrument for world peace, and his ecumenical passion increased as the Second World War became more likely.

## TEMPLE'S THEOLOGICAL WRITINGS

At only one stage in his career was Temple clearly identified with a 'modernising' theology of a radical kind. This was when he was still at Repton. He contributed an essay on 'The Divinity of Christ' to Foundations (1912), a symposium which was edited by the liberal theologian B. H. Streeter. Temple was publicly attacked in 1913 by Ronald Knox, then still a High Anglican traditionalist at Oxford, but soon to become a Roman Catholic, in a book called Some Loose Stones, which rejected the whole liberal tendency as illustrated by Foundations.

There is a widespread myth that Some Loose Stones was a devastatingly witty attack on Temple. More relevant is the way in which the two books demonstrated the gap between the theological 'modernisers' and their opponents and so help to explain why Temple constantly sought to provide Anglicanism with a firmer intellectual base. If one clears away the rhetoric of the combatants, what Temple was saying was that one could believe in a direct, even an absolute, relationship between Jesus and God, but that the notions of the Virgin Birth and the Resurrection of Jesus' body, which the churches had certainly taught in the past, no longer positively helped in making sense of belief in the divinity of Christ. Knox, on the other hand, was claiming that the true church could not cease to teach what it had taught in the past about the Virgin Birth and the Resurrection of Jesus' body – that these were historical events – and that being a Christian involved obedience to the church's dogmatic authority.

Knox said that Modernism, 'like Latitudinarianism, is based on a tendency, the tendency to be up to date' (Knox, 1913, p. 214). He illustrated this by saying, mistakenly, that Temple's view of the Incarnation was derived from Henri Bergson, a French philosopher fashionable at the time. The Modernist 'critical' approach was, according to Knox, out of place in Christian theology, 'because we are only the trustees of tradition' (p. 215). He prophesied, more correctly this time, a reaction against the New Testament 'critics', saying that 'the Enlightenment of the nineteenth century has not yet spent its force; but if I am not mistaken, there will be a reckoning' (p. 215). This showed the real basis of Knox's position: he was rejecting not just 'Modernist' biblical criticism but the mainstream of Western thought and experience since the eighteenth century. It was not simply a question of refusing to be 'up to date': Knox wanted to summon up the spirits of the Ancien Régime and re-establish Christian dogma as absolute truth.

As far as the doctrine of the divinity of Christ was concerned Knox argued from a high metaphysical definition of 'God' to an interpretation of Jesus. Temple, however, as

Knox understood him, was saying that we should look first at the character of Jesus for our conception of the divine. This meant, Knox argued, that Temple no longer regarded the Jesus of the New Testament as 'omnipotent or omniscient' (Knox, 1913, p. 98). Knox himself answered the question: On what authority did one say that Jesus was divine? by attributing to the 'church' the authority to declare that this was so: one had then to read the New Testament in accordance with this prior ecclesiastical pronouncement. His case for the omniscience of Christ, for example, was that 'the Church teaches me he was God all the time, and I cannot think away from God his attributes of perfect power, wisdom and goodness' (p. 108). In Jesus, he claimed, the dogmatic definition was clear: 'two separate functions of willing, one a human function and the other a divine function, were conjoined by a process which metaphysics are unable to explain or even express' (p. 153). How one could understand what one could not express he did not say.

Knox also challenged Temple's orthodoxy over the doctrine of the Second Coming of Christ. He said that he himself believed that 'at any one moment, quite as much as another, the odds are, from my point of view, that the heavens will be literally rent asunder, that creation will really begin to throb with the birth-throes of a new existence, and that into that new mode of existence I, with all those now living on earth, will be caught up without warning, to give account of my works. But I doubt if the modern theologian really regards this possibility as a possibility' (Knox, 1913, p. 110). One doubts if Knox himself really held this position as existentially as he claimed, but he asserted that 'the present headmaster of Repton' quarrelled not just with the apparent dating of the Day of Judgement in the gospels but with the whole spirit and machinery of it – 'the whole thing is a mere piece of Oriental imagery' (p. 114). Historically, however,

Temple's attitude was closer to Anglican tradition than Knox's.

The case for theological modernisation, according to Temple's understanding of the difficulties of many of his contemporaries in the Church of England, was that the kind of theological system which Knox was putting forward, and the attitude to the New Testament which it required, were no longer either plausible or compelling. No doubt in the past there had been a Christian community which had told the New Testament stories uncritically and which had fervently expected, for example, the imminent snapping off of historical time before a once-for-all Final Judgement, but one could not live as though there had been no 'nineteenth-century Enlightenment', or as though the Western mind had been on a totally wrong track since about 1700, if not since the early sixteenth century.

Temple replied to Knox in a letter (29 October 1913: see Iremonger, 1948, pp. 161–6), in which he stressed the differences between them. His fundamental assertion was that he did not believe 'in the ideal of a Church with sharply defined [dogmatic] boundaries' (p. 162): in other words, he rejected Knox's authoritarian view of the church's dogmatic authority. He had, he said, no presupposition against miracles, and he was therefore prepared to believe in the Virgin Birth, but he could not 'find any real theological significance in it' – a rider which blew a great hole in conservative theology. He added that 'I believe in our Lord's Bodily Resurrection, but if it could (*per impossibile*) be disproved, I don't think it would affect my faith as a whole' (p. 163). Such qualifications limited the force of his statement that he did not see clearly any point at which the church's dogmatic teaching was actually 'wrong', because they implied a wide margin in which it could hardly be said that the church was 'right'.

He admitted that Knox was correct in supposing that he did not expect an imminent, catastrophic end of the world – 'though of course I do not dream of denying its possibility', an addition which had its convenient side – 'but then I am quite convinced that our Lord himself did not expect it' (p. 163). Here he was less qualified in his conclusion, emphasising what Knox did not want to grant where dogma was concerned, that more than one interpretation of the New Testament text was possible: 'I think our Lord definitely rejected the apocalyptic idea of the Messiahship' (p. 164). More significantly, he added that 'if I thought he expected an immediate catastrophe other than his own death and resurrection, I think I should have to renounce Christianity' (p. 164). Many radical New Testament critics of the early twentieth century shared the opinion that one could not take Jesus seriously if his theology turned on a literal Second Coming, and many, like Temple, solved the problem by reading the evidence to mean that Jesus rejected such ideas.

Temple, therefore, clearly felt that what was needed by the Church of England in the new century was a set of guidelines to possible belief rather than a precise dogmatic system of the traditional type. One should allow people the chance of regarding themselves as 'Christian', and rather than looking for theological definitions which would exclude the hesitant, give them time to work out their own statement of faith. He defended the Anglican 'Modernists' by conducting a cautious retreat from history as far as such ideas as the Virgin Birth and the Bodily Resurrection of Jesus were concerned. These ideas had no significant symbolic value for him – their historicity as 'events' was of no account because even if such 'events' had taken place, they would have been theologically irrelevant. And the idea that Jesus had taught that there was to be an imminent winding up of history in a 'Second Advent' struck him as grounds for giving up Christianity, because it would expose too cruelly the limitations of Jesus' religious imagination for one to persevere with the ascription of 'divinity'. Temple was left with the problem that he still wanted to affirm the divinity of Jesus. His solution was to approach the question of divinity from the picture of Jesus given in the gospels. This meant that his exposition of 'the divinity of Jesus' was not charged with the heavy load of dogmatic ideas which Knox accepted because the church taught them. Temple argued that 'God is Jesus-like, and that is to me, and I believe always has been for the Church, the primary import of the incarnation' (p. 165). His statement in 1913 pointed forward to his attitude as chairman of the postwar Anglican Committee on Doctrine. Its report, published in 1938, declined to make final pronouncements on disputed doctrinal issues, but simply recorded the conflicting viewpoints of liberals, Evangelicals and Anglo-Catholics and asserted that Anglicans were entitled to hold any of them.

How far did Temple's specific anxieties appear in print? When in the same year (1913) he published his Repton School Sermons, which were sub-titled 'Studies in the religion of the incarnation', he had been criticised by the Oxford Magazine for 'uncritical preaching', and throughout his life he sometimes wrote and preached as though Christianity offered no intellectual difficulties at all. The late Readings in St. John's Gospel (2 vols. 1939 and 1940) were very popular precisely because they gave the impression that difficulties had been overcome – 'Why anyone should have troubled to crucify the Christ of Liberal Protestantism has always been a mystery', he mildly noted (Temple, 1939, p. xxiv).

The same kind of criticism cannot, however, be made of his article in Foundations. There is no mention of the doctrine of the Virgin Birth. Instead, Temple's reconstruction of the life of Jesus (Temple, 1914a, p. 260–3) starts from a later point: 'We watch the Lord as he becomes conscious at his baptism that he is entrusted with a mission which must be called messianic if it is to be expressed in words at all: he goes into the wilderness to meet the temptations which arise from this conviction' (p. 260). Knox made much of the fact that the index of Foundations did not even refer to Bethlehem, Birth, Joseph, Mary, Nativity or Virgin, but there was no question of Temple's concealing anything: the editing of Foundations made it clear that the Virgin Birth was regarded as peripheral, and all the essays had been written on the basis of Mark's Gospel and the Pauline writings. In the case of the Resurrection Temple seemed to have accepted the Streeter position that there was a glorified body, even if the tomb would naturally have been empty.

In Mens Creatrix (1917), there is a chapter on 'The Word Incarnate' (c. 23, pp. 311–23). Here again there was no mention of Mary or virginity, but Temple took his line from the Gospel of St John and expanded it philosophically in his own idealist manner. 'The Lord is here set forth not merely as the promised Messiah but as the manifestation once for all of the eternal principle which governs the universe. The Logos . . . stood for that over-ruling and unifying principle which the mind must inevitably presuppose when it starts upon its work of explaining the world in which we live' (Temple, 1917, pp. 316–17). It is clear that Temple thought of the figure of Jesus in the gospel as somehow revealing this 'principle' or 'process'. 'We cannot think of the world as something which, even for a moment, moves independently of God, and which God intervenes to correct or adjust; but neither on the other hand can we think of the world-process in anything less than its entirety as supplying an exposition of the divine purpose in Christ. Only in the life of Christ is this manifestation given. What we see in him is what we should see in the history of the universe if we could apprehend that history in its completeness' (pp. 317–18).

One begins to see the nature and perhaps the force of Knox's objection from the Catholic side. There is no question but that Temple believed that in the Palestinian life of Jesus the historical purposive-process revealed itself – this was the way in which Temple could, in the tradition of Hegel, accept the idea of revelation. He believed in God and in God's self-revelation. He was prepared to say that what we knew about God as personality depended on what Jesus showed of him in this revelatory life. What is not so clear is what he made of the Palestinian figure of Jesus: was this a man, momentarily taken up into the universal principle, or was this a human equivalent of the universal principle, or what? Knox argued that to say that it was only in Christ that we had any clear image of God was to say only that Jesus was like Jesus: in his reply to Knox Temple said that one could surely say that 'God is Jesus-like' (Iremonger, 1948, p. 165), and that this was different. At the same time, Temple said in Foundations (pp. 258–9) that we learned what humanity was by looking at Christ, because we did not know what humanity was or of what achievements it was capable, until divinity (the purpose-process) indwelled it. Temple went on, quite lyrically, to say that when man was thus united to God, 'Nature is his servant, not his master, and he may (so the story tells us) walk upon the water; the fetters of social influence cannot bind him, and he may be sinless, though tempted, in a sinful world' (Streeter, 1912, p. 259). In the published essay the introduction of the 'so the story tells' is a weak face-saving device which leaves the status of the 'miracle' ambiguous, but in the letter to Knox, Temple said outright that he believed Christ walked on water.

The upshot was that Knox wanted a 'Jesus' who was virginally 'born' as an appropriate vehicle for divinity. Temple implied that this approach was unnecessary, that Jesus was born in the usual way, that his body would have been in the tomb in the usual way but for circumstances which are likely to remain unknown to us, but that in Jesus' living person God demonstrated or revealed both the potentialities of man and the personality of God. A glorified body was possible, not because (as Knox said) the virginally conceived body was incapable of corruption, but because this newly achieved unity of the divine and the human did not cease at death.

In the article in Foundations on the divinity of Christ, Temple again showed that socio-political questions were his major interest. He said, for example, that human beings were 'social through and through. Modern thought is only just returning from the exaggerated protest of individualism to a just appreciation of the fact which was the basis of Greek political thought, the fact that we are born members of our families, of our nations, of our race, and that all are linked together with bonds of mutual sympathy and influence' (pp. 253–4). Jesus as divine-human was related to this organic humanity.

Temple's full-scale answer to those who doubted his belief in the orthodox doctrine of the Incarnation was offered in Mens Creatrix, published in 1917 during the Great War. Starting from the assumption of faith in God as holy and righteous will, he tried to show that this approach made the facts of experience more intelligible than any other. He turned away from biblical criticism to metaphysics, and tried to show that various elements of modern thought, epistemology, aesthetics, politics and philosophy of religion were moving on converging lines towards unity in the dogma of the Incarnation. This was a bold, if essentially hopeless, attempt to reassert the primacy of Christian dogma in Western culture, and to overcome the loss of confidence caused by the decline in the authority of both the biblical text and the churches themselves. Temple spoke of the decline of

'Christendom' in the face of nationalism, a process which had begun in the sixteenth century, but which in 1917 he thought, wrongly, might be reversed by the internationalism which he believed was being generated by the Great War.

Once again, Temple was reflecting the mood of a generation which desperately wanted to see good coming out of so much destruction. When he said that 'Christendom' was precisely the world as no longer alien, 'but as seeking to conduct its secular affairs in the power of that life of which the Church is the channel and trustee' (Temple, 1917, p. 326), he was well aware that he was not describing the West as it was in 1917, or, perhaps, the West as it had been in the fifteenth and sixteenth centuries, but that he was stating an ideal relationship between the divine and the human and calling it 'Christendom'. 'Christendom', in fact, became his gloss on 'church establishment', and along this line of argument 'establishment' was neither a political convenience for the state nor a threat to religious liberty for the citizen, but an institution theologically necessary in order to implement the divine will. He suggested the formula of 'the free state within the free Church' (p. 329), a deliberate reversal of the more secular Victorian Nonconformist slogan: 'a free Church in a free state'. The only permanent, because religious, solution to nationalism was that modern states should come to recognise themselves as provinces in the spiritual Kingdom of Christ, deriving their welfare from the welfare of the whole Kingdom of God. Temple explicitly said that the energy which created and sustained the nation-states was that of the Divine Spirit, for nation-states, 'in our modern jargon, are the operation of God immanent in history, while the life of the Church is the energy of God transcendent' (p. 324). This was a full-blooded declaration of faith that the Christian dogmatic system could explain even the detail of history as part of a divine creative purpose. This position was to be clarified in the less persuasive, more purely Christian, argument of *Christus Veritas* in 1924.

There was a weakness in his method, however, because his philosophical argument did not necessarily point towards a personal creator revealed by Jesus but towards an immanent, impersonal, universal order, an unapproachable metaphysical absolutism which did not need to be underwritten by a specific written revelation of the Christian kind. In *Mens Creatrix*, on the contrary, Temple was committed to defending the idea of a personal creator, as distinct from an impersonal system. He needed a more sensitive image for God than 'the Absolute', and turned especially to aesthetic images. He suggested that just as an artist might say that he painted a picture in order 'to create a thing of beauty for the delight of myself and others' (p. 89), so God might be thought of as creating the universe with the purpose of achieving good. That would be the kind of explanation which would satisfy our minds, whereas an immanent order might simply be an ultimate fact, to be accepted. In 1917 Temple admitted that the intellect might be satisfied with the contemplation of impersonal order as such, either present or evolving, but in *Nature, Man and God* (1934), his last major theological essay, he withdrew this concession.

Temple argued that the life of Jesus (the Incarnation) could be defined satisfactorily as the way in which the invisible but personal God offered a revelation of himself, a description of his spiritual features and purposes. As in 1913, Temple saw no gain in giving an elaborate explanation of how this event took place; the doctrines of the Virgin Birth and the Resurrection of Jesus' body he set on one side as adding nothing to theology. Instead, he concentrated on the 'meaning' of the Incarnation, its effect – through our knowledge of Jesus – on our knowledge and experience of God. Given the Incarnation as the meeting-place of human and divine, Temple treated the 'atonement' in the same way. He was at his most orthodox in his acceptance of the classical Christian view that a 'fallen' creation had become separated from its creator, so that, in the jargon, a 'new creation' was necessary. The atonement made this new creation possible.

In Mens Creatrix therefore, the Christian dogmatic system was largely taken for granted and interpreted in philosophical terms. Theological talk of 'salvation' was presented in terms of 'development', of change which was being brought about in historical time by a divine process initiated and sustained by the Incarnation, the atonement and the consequent foundation of the church, which for Temple was essentially a supernatural institution, visibly present in bodies like the Church of England. He did his best to produce a synthesis between the philosophers and the theologians, and for some years after the publication of Mens Creatrix he still thought that the dominant trend in philosophy was 'spiritual and theistic', that a Christocentric metaphysics could hold the centre of the stage (Iremonger, 1948, p. 521). This was an error of judgement: one may take the publication of an English translation of Wittgenstein's Tractatus Logico-Philosophicus in 1922 as a sign of a broad shift in British philosophy from idealism back to empiricism. The parallel in the Christian sub-culture was a widespread distrust of philosophy and a renewed attempt in the 1930s to present the Bible as a unique and self-authenticating revelation of the mind of God. Younger religious writers refused to interpret contemporary events as more than signs of a chaos which God would resolve in a Final Judgement. In the totalitarian period Christian pessimism and pacificism frequently combined. There were short-lived theological demands for a return to the Reformation, on the one hand, and to a suitably modified medievalism on the other. With this climatic change (it was hardly intellectual) Temple had only limited sympathy. In

June 1944, only four months before his death, he wrote, in
*Christianity as an Interpretation of History*:

We must work, we must strive and prepare for the coming of the
kingdom in this world; but we must recognize that the first form of
its appearance will not be the already perfect achievement of love,
but the establishment of justice between what are still fundamentally self-centred wills and groups of wills rather than the
relationship of pure love. If we can get that far, we shall at least have
gone a very long way from where we stand at this moment. (p. 21)

Temple retained, that is, his theological conviction that the
divine purpose of Christianity extended beyond the individual to the creation of a morally just society. When the
philosopher A. E. Taylor reviewed *Mens Creatrix* in *Mind* in
1917, he reacted strongly against Temple's position and said
that 'Mr Temple, like all Anglo-Hegelians, is anxious to exalt
the "State" at the cost of the individual, and follows the usual
line of insisting that all obligation is social obligation.' He
also sharply resisted Temple's assertion that one should make
the world a better place, 'even if you have to do dirty work in
the process' (Temple, 1917, p. 193). Taylor commented:

I have not much sympathy with the attitude of even the most honest
of our present 'conscientious objectors', because I think their
'consciences' curiously unenlightened, but the temper displayed
towards the little minority in this matter by the Northcliffe
newspapers and the ignorant crowd who take their opinions from
my Lord Northcliffe and his puppets leads me to think with Lord
Hugh Cecil that society, at the present moment, needs no warning
against overconscientiousness, but rather the reverse. We are in
serious danger of relapsing into the mob persecution and possibly
the legal persecution of minorities who refuse to regard the
commands of a legislature which is rapidly sinking into the
condition of a mere board for registering the decrees of a ring of
unscrupulous financiers and press-men, as the ultimate authority in
morals, and a moral philosophy like Mr Temple's is only helping to

bring the danger nearer . . . While actual 'society' remains in matters of conduct what it too often shows itself to be, a mere blustering bully, it is good for society itself that some persons should refuse to fall down and worship. (Taylor, 1917, p. 227)

Taylor was surely right in saying that one might profoundly and properly reject the nature of the society in which one found oneself, and have no inclination to serve it. Temple, who was never a conscientious objector himself but who defended the civil rights of objectors, found it easy enough to accept the comfortable English environment which he knew, but even so he himself rejected the nature of Western capitalism in 1918 on the basis of his own theory about what the divine purpose for industrial society might be. How far Temple was prepared to go in compelling people to accept a 'divine society' was never clear, partly because political possibilities ran consistently in the opposite direction for most of his life. Taylor was more alarmed than he was at the growth of the power both of the wartime British state and of mass opinion, and thought that Temple's theology fitted these developments too closely. In political terms, the prospect of 'a free state within a free Church' was menacing because it underestimated the attractions of power, not least to ecclesiastics.

To be fair, one needs to look at Temple's ideas in a wider context. Already in the 1920s in Europe there was widespread alarm in many countries at the loss of an agreed set of common values which had, it was believed, cemented society together in the past. There was much talk, in styles not dissimilar from Temple's, of the need to reaffirm 'the organic unity' of the community, though there was little agreement about what the spiritual centre of this unity should be. There was no strong desire to restore to the churches the authority over society which had been removed from them in the nineteenth century. As far as the churches themselves were concerned, there was no simple European equivalent for Temple's drive to revive the Anglican establishment as a way of promoting social cohesion, though German Protestantism in the Weimar period (the 1920s) and Roman Catholicism in Republican Spain before the outbreak of the Civil War (1936) both suffered an acute feeling of loss of social power which was the equivalent of the loss of an established position. In practice, the political movements which made most play with ideas of 'organic unity' were the Fascists and Nazis, and their success discredited the concept in many ways, weakening the churches at the same time because both Catholics and Protestants were attracted to these totalitarian movements when they attacked Communism and seemed to defend conservative sexual ethics.

Temple could write from this point of view. In *Mens Creatrix*, for example, he deplored the fact, which he attributed to the influence of the Roman Catholic Church, that

religion in the West has tended to become individualist almost in the degree in which it is spiritual. Before there can be again such a thing as Christendom existing in the world as a living fact, we must recover . . . the idea of a moral and spiritual corporate life which, if not the whole end of man is none the less part of his end, and therefore to be regarded in proper proportion as a true end in itself. *For this purpose we must first realise the spiritual character of the State even in its most material functions.* (p. 330, my italics)

When Temple speaks of 'the spiritual character of the State even in its most material functions', one realises how remote his political assumptions were from those which had governed the development of the modern British state, which now increasingly behaved as though it were an acceptable alternative to 'Christendom'. He himself was drawing on his philosophical background to offer intellectual support to the High Anglican tradition which argued that the ideal state would disseminate a Christian world-view, against which all social claims to meaning and value could be tested. At the practical level, such ideas explained Temple's stubborn defence of the churches' part in British education in the 1940s, as well as his view that religious broadcasting stood on a different footing from anything else that the BBC, then still a monopoly, provided, and should be controlled by the churches.

As early as *Mens Creatrix*, where the political theme was already the most exciting part of the argument, what distinguished Temple from politically conservative religious writers was that his theological version of 'organic unity' became a justification of what we have come to call the 'Welfare State'. In his view to set up a society organised to look after the whole population as far as provision for health, work, education, housing and old age was concerned would be to express the will of God in terms of social justice. In *Mens Creatrix* he took for granted that the final victory of the ideas of equality and cooperation over those of acquisitiveness and competition was to be interpreted as progress to a higher stage of human existence. This programme did not mean, in his opinion, substituting socialist politics for the Christian gospel, but moving away from secular politics towards the politics of the Kingdom of God. In practice the British Welfare State was set up in the late 1940s by the accident of war which briefly made radical innovation possible. Despite Temple's efforts there was no strong theoretical commitment to a supporting ideology, either secular or religious, and those who wanted to attack the Welfare State in later years did not have to make their case against a major theological defence.

In *Nature, Man and God*, the Gifford Lectures of 1932–4, Temple dropped the political theme for the moment, and tried once more to give Christianity a secure basis in modern culture, philosophical, scientific and aesthetic. In theory the

Giffords were supposed to be about philosophy of religion, not theology, and his aim was to show that a world in which independent human minds and wills occurred was only explicable in terms of a supernatural Mind and Purpose, on which this world and human minds depended for their existence. Temple himself went further, saying that his argument reconciled this rather grey theism to a conception of the world 'as grounded in the creative purpose of the living God who fulfils himself in the fulfilment of that purpose' (Temple, 1934, p. xxxi). The use of the biblical phrase 'the living God' implied that Temple had successfully shown a connexion between philosophical theism and the God of the Christian tradition, but few commentators have accepted this claim.

One of Temple's weaknesses as a Christian philosopher of religion was that he could not conceive of a serious religious alternative to Christianity; he shared the essentially dismissive reaction of Christian writers in the 1930s to the possibility of any re-emergence of other world religions from the marginal, shrinking role which they had been allotted by the West in the nineteenth century. He understood the need (which was really defensive) to unite Christian missions in the ecumenical movement, but he did not question the missionary duty of Christianity to replace other world religions, and he found no need to go beyond Christianity in a discussion of the concept of 'religion'. Yet already in 1934 a secular reviewer like E. W. Edwards could complain that Temple defined 'religion' so as to exclude 'the religions of the Way which do not need, as his does, a Creator or dependence on a Supreme Reality or Will' (Edwards, 1934, p. 240).

Temple, like virtually all his theological contemporaries, lacked a sense of the singularity of the principal Christian dogmas, such as the Incarnation, Resurrection, Original Sin and the Trinity. Basic Christian assumptions, that Jesus revealed 'what God was like', for example, that the 'atonement' was both necessary and intelligible, that a kind of self-negation or auto-destruction of the self was what God demanded from each human being, that the 'church' was a divinely established institution in the forms (especially the 'catholic' episcopal form) in which it existed in his lifetime – Temple took these theological positions for granted as though the system they constituted was self-authenticating. He recognised, however, that after more than a century of conflict, the tension between understanding the Bible as a historically conditioned text ('biblical criticism') and under-standing the Bible as the God-given authority of the twentieth-century church ('revelation') could no longer be resolved: 'biblical criticism' had no more to offer to Christianity, and the authority of 'revelation' could no longer be demonstrated by the church. Temple's own solution, like that of many of his theological contemporaries, was to argue that the free-floating Christian dogmatic system which survived was confirmed by human religious experience. This was what he tried to show in *Nature, Man and God*, and it had the ironical result that his case for the existence of a Personal Deity was better than his case for Christianity.

By setting Christian dogmas in the context of a confident philosophy of religion no doubt he comforted some of his more anxious Christian contemporaries. There was an understandable error, however, in the judgement of men like Temple and J. H. Oldham, who were convinced by the time of the Oxford Conference on 'Church, Community and State' in 1937 that Christianity must defend itself above all against the encroachment of great secular systems like Communism, Fascism and Nazism. These undoubtedly hostile forces were to disintegrate before the end of the twentieth century, without the churches having done much to cause their decline. The alternative world religions, on the other hand, survived and encroached steadily on the boundaries of Western culture, without the churches having learned much more about them than they knew before the Second World War. In the long run Temple's own theological critique of Western capitalism was more significant than his work in the philosophy of religion.

When he wrote *Nature, Man and God* Temple was well aware that his assertions about 'the creative purpose of the living God' clashed with the apparent chaos of existence. Like many people in 1930s he thought of the human race as having 'evolved', but he could not accept an account of biological evolution which did not embrace the idea of Man as 'fallen' and 'redeemed'. His picture of how human evolution had taken place – of human beings gradually learning to control themselves and their environment, at first inevitably from their own individual and finite point of view, but moving slowly towards the possibility of association for the apparent common good – did not in itself warrant the introduction of classical Christian language about the Fall and Original Sin, and the need for Redemption. At his most dogmatic Temple invoked the darker side of the Christian tradition, saying that 'it is the spirit which is evil, it is reason which is perverted; it is aspiration itself which is corrupt' (Temple, 1934, p. 368), but this was gratuitous.

'What is wanted,' Temple argued, 'is some ground for belief that the occurrence of the evil is an actual element in the total good' (p. 508). He started from Bosanquet, who had said that the answer of Christianity to the idea of the Fall would be that the scheme of salvation, involving finiteness and sin, was essential to the nature of God and the perfection of the universe (p. 509). Temple argued that the good of the universe was greater because of the evil which had to be overcome. After the Holocaust and the atom-bombing of

Hiroshima and Nagasaki, the argument lacks compelling force.

Temple was writing in the mid 1930s, however, and despite the contemporary awareness of the suffering caused by the First World War still felt able to say that

God accepted the occurrence of evil as a consequence of the principle of creation which he adopted and . . . therefore its occurrence falls within, and not outside, the divine plan. No doubt the evil is in a most true sense contrary to God's will; for it is the taking by a finite will of its own way in preference to God's. Yet it must be regarded as falling within the divine purpose that finite spirits should make choices contrary to that purpose. No man who chooses evil can justly plead – 'God willed me so to choose', for the essence of his evil choice is that it is a rejection of God's will for him. But he can plead, and his moral health depends upon his recognising, that God has made him and all men such that if they follow their own apparent good without reference to God, they will act contrary to God's will and to their own real good. This is, we have suggested, the vital truth and importance of Original Sin. (pp. 501–2)

What Temple was clinging to was his belief that everything fell 'within the divine purpose', and he restated his position by making the apparent human insolubility of the problem of evil its solution. On the one hand, he said, 'only in genuine mutual love is there release from the evils of the world'. Men half-understood that, and tried to live in that way, but on the other hand they were also partly driven by motives which prevented the perfecting of mutual love. He gave a shrewd political example:

Communism seeks to create by force a world of mutual cooperation, believing that those who grow up in such a world will be freed from acquisitiveness and self-concern. But the effect will only be to direct those motives upon other objects than wealth, such as honour and influence. And the initial trust in force, which is always an appeal to self-concern, will stimulate the sentiment which it aims at destroying. Man cannot meet his own deepest need, nor find for himself release from his own deepest trouble. What he needs is not progress, but redemption. If the Kingdom of God is to come on earth, it must be because God first comes on earth himself. (p. 513)

The ponderous language of Edwardian theology, heavily in debt to the Victorian pulpit, rumbled on, but here Temple was dissociating himself from liberal theologians like F. R. Tennant, who sharply opposed the orthodox idea, which Temple seemed at times to accept, of a bias towards evil in human nature. In this respect, Temple cannot be called a liberal theologian. *Nature, Man and God* culminated in the assertion that only the self-revelation of the divine as utterly selfless love in the form of Jesus, who is also a 'finite self whose apparent good is also the real good', wins 'the submission of the conscience, the subjection of the will, the adoration of the heart . . .'. This event opened a way to communion with God. 'All is of God; the only thing of my very own which I can contribute to my own redemption is the sin from which I need to be redeemed' (Temple, 1934, p. 401). As Edwards commented in his review: 'How such a mere lack, or fragment, of being can sin is not discussed. On the contrary the Archbishop boldly winds up the discussion with: "We are clay in the hands of the potter" (402), thus finally asserting that view of men as things which he emphatically repudiated when facing naturalistic determinism' (Edwards, 1934, p. 242). This criticism was echoed by J. F. Padgett, who said that one could not eliminate the human self in Temple's theological fashion and then leave it to the mercy of God mysteriously to restore the self undamaged and somehow free (Padgett, 1974, pp. 275–8).

Always political, in the sense that he was never satisfied with a theology of the individual, Temple also considered the problem of evil in relation to the desire of human beings to create civilisations and states. In 1934 he modified the view of *Mens Creatrix* that states were part of the divine order, and said that civilisation, which created the state as a controller of force in the service of law, in order to prevent the lawless use of force, was bound to become corrupt through the need to exercise force at all (Temple, 1934, p. 505). One is reminded of the German sociologist Max Weber's comment that it was hard to envisage a Christian politics, precisely because force had to be tolerated as part of the political reality. As in 1917, however, Temple did not surrender to despair. 'Neither by monasticism alone, wherein man seeks to withdraw from the contamination of the world, nor by quixotic idealism alone . . . is the transformation of actual to ideal forwarded . . . but mostly the transformation is to be effected by those who, being in their own minds conformed to the ideal, act upon the actual according to its capacity of response' (p. 506).

This was another statement of the position which he always held, that the religious man had to take the risk of working within a corrupted system, with whatever likelihood of being socially destructive, for the sake of the possibility of doing some good. Even so, and despite his efforts to serve the 'divine purpose', the reforming politician would not escape corruption. Theologically, this had to be taken for granted: man was 'born in sin' and 'a child of wrath', he said; 'original sin' was an 'indubitable fact' which 'coheres with our general account of the world process and of man's place in it' (p. 370). As a result, civilisation and culture were riddled with selfishness, and only the Mind and Purpose behind creation, acting through Jesus, could enable humanity to build a harmonious system.

Orthodoxy, a little muddled, but orthodoxy still, dominated Temple's political theology in its abstract form, and made an adverse judgement of human history inevitable. He gave a fair account of human growth in self-awareness and grasp of the environment, a growth which left people self-centred and therefore, since they were also equipped with imagination and will, prone to self-regarding choices which conflicted with the choices of others in a destructive way. At his most Hegelian in 1934, he could say that 'the persons or selves which occur in the World Process are finite . . . their own well-being is dependent on the principle of the Whole in which they are no more than episodes' (p. 368). This was not a specifically Christian world-view. To produce one, Temple imposed on the story of human evolution a traditional Christian psychology of man and with it a drastic Christian moral judgement on human nature. Hence the emphasis on original sin, which he gave a historical gloss by saying that 'it is not wicked to be finite; but it is so improbable as to be beyond all reasonable estimate of practical possibility that finite selves, if left to themselves, should not be wicked' (p. 369).

Here Temple seems to contradict himself. Given that what we had in historical time and space was 'finite selves . . . left to themselves . . .', and given people's unpredictable mixture of self-centred and associative tendencies (which, as F. R. Tennant said, would make the idea of a bias towards good as reasonable as the idea of a bias towards evil), what overwhelming need was there to interpret the historical outcome in terms of 'Original Sin', 'the Fall of Man' and the need for 'Redemption', which last could be obtained only if the self were uprooted from its 'Selfcentre', and drawn to find its centre in God, the Spirit of the Whole? This was a return to the assumptions of biblical 'sacred history' as opposed to 'histoire raisonnée'. Nor did Temple's discussion justify him in saying that human nature is far gone in corruption and perversion (Temple, 1934, p. 376). The most that Temple showed was that on his theistic hypothesis the

God involved had had to accept the mixed outcome of his efforts at creation, and had found no simple way of strengthening people's moral and social balance. He came closer than he imagined to the position of Rashdall, in *The Theory of Good and Evil*, who had suggested that only the concept of a 'finite' Deity offered a solution.

## LIFE AND LIBERTY

In discussing Life and Liberty, a movement which, during the First World War, briefly pursued the almost complete separation of the English church and state, one has to remember that a Liberal government had in 1912 introduced legislation to disestablish the church in Wales; this had become law in 1914, though its application was delayed until the Great War ended. As Archbishop of Canterbury, Davidson had opposed the measure desperately, and his defeat goes some way to explain his anxiety about Life and Liberty, which briefly looked as though it might challenge establishment as such. The Welsh case for disestablishment had rested firmly on nationalist grounds: the Church of England was 'alien' in Wales, and the majority of Welsh people did not belong to it. The nationalist argument could not easily be transferred to England, but Davidson must have been shaken by the public readiness of men like Temple to say that if disestablishment was the price that had to be paid for Anglican self-government, he and others were ready to pay it. Another prominent figure in Life and Liberty was the Anglo-Catholic leader Charles Gore, Bishop of Oxford from 1911, who had been one of only three bishops who had supported the Welsh measure: Gore went further than Temple and supported disestablishment in England as well.

Life and Liberty involved a brief struggle – it lasted from 1917 to 1919 – for the future direction of the Church of

England which Temple, as the accepted leader of the movement, could have won only if he had been the kind of dominant personality that some of his admirers always told themselves that he was. The truth, which recent historians of the Church of England have been loath to admit, is that Anglicanism had become too deeply divided in the course of the nineteenth century for any individual to unite it in the way that Temple was expected to do. Hensley Henson partly grasped this at the time, when he contrasted a group of reformers concerned about the establishment's efficiency with another, largely Anglo-Catholic, group, which was above all anxious that its own theological definition of Anglicanism should not be obscured by the connexion with the state, and which talked about the need for 'spiritual independence'. As Henson observed, the two groups could not pull indefinitely in the same direction. Kenneth Thompson's sociological study, *Bureaucracy and Church Reform* (1970), exploited a similar insight into what happened, arguing that there was bound to be conflict between the idea of an efficient, bureaucratic church on the one hand, and the vision of a spiritually free ecclesiastical community on the other.

This was a highly public dispute which should not be thought of purely in terms of the eventual setting-up of the Church Assembly, although this was a gain for the partisans of efficiency. It was clear before 1914 that the administrative machinery of the establishment needed overhaul, but the church could be changed significantly only through Parliament, and a busier and more secular House of Commons had become disinclined to spare the time, so that between 1880 and 1913 183 out of 217 church bills introduced into the House had been dropped. The Archbishops set up a committee of their own in 1913 to consider what changes were advisable 'in order to secure in the relations of Church and State a fuller expression of the spiritual independence of the Church as well as of the national recognition of religion'. This committee's report, published in 1917, recommended the introduction of what became the Church Assembly, an institutional innovation which would probably have taken place, for purely practical reasons, without the war and also, one suspects, without the Life and Liberty movement. There is some exaggeration in E. R. Norman's assertion (Norman, 1976, p. 275) that the social radicalism associated with Life and Liberty made people suspicious of the demand for Anglican autonomy. The Selborne Report, as it may be called after the title of its chairman, the Earl of Selborne, and the legislation which followed from it after the war did not, however, settle the question of 'spiritual independence' from the state, but left final power still in the hands of Crown and Parliament. This was dramatically illustrated in 1927/8, when proposals for a revision of the Anglican Prayer Book were firmly rejected twice in the House of Commons. Temple was a junior member of the Selborne Committee and was therefore aware of the way in which the mind of its cautious majority was moving.

Questions of independence and efficiency did not exhaust what was at issue. When Welsh disestablishment was being debated in the House of Commons in the summer of 1912, one of Temple's older mentors, Scott Holland, had noted in his Anglo-Catholic review *The Commonwealth* two rival pictures of what 'establishment' meant. Arthur Balfour, Conservative politician and occasional philosopher, had described Anglicanism as the ideal home of the anxious intellectual, because it was sympathetic and took long views of passing disputes: a disestablished Anglican sect would never be so gentle and wise. Holland was amused but preferred the Liberal Charles Masterman, who had replied that it was all very well for the establishment to be tolerant of long drawn-out philosophical uncertainty, but judicious compromise in the face of social wrong was the sin of sins: when had the establishment ever lifted the flag of social justice or freedom (Holland, 1912, p. 178)?

It was this broader anxiety about the proper relationship between the Church of England, established or disestablished, and the society which the nineteenth century had created, which found expression through Life and Liberty. The Great War had a devastating, if rather transient, effect on many Anglican clergy, who found that the war, while it lasted, gave an unexpected point and pathos to their existence as priests: for once they seemed to themselves to be connecting with the vital experience of ordinary people. They were not sure what should be done, but they did not want this sense of belonging to an institution which seemed truly to be 'the Church of the English people' to fade into nothing; some of them suffered acutely when that happened quite quickly after the Armistice. They were also affected by their discovery that for the ordinary British soldier Christianity was no longer even a 'folk-religion': the local church and Sunday-school system in which the clergy of all denominations had trusted was not working: neither belief in nor knowledge of the details of Christianity was being handed on.

The initial religious (as distinct from political-patriotic) response of the clergy to war had been to talk about the need for national repentance, and many of them would have preferred to stick to that religiously irreproachable position. Temple shared the general clerical feeling that although Germany was no doubt to blame for the war, the British ought to repent of their materialistic misuse of the peaceful years which had preceded it. It is not clear why the average housewife, nurse, miner or doctor should have felt particularly convinced by this campaign, and it was hardly surprising that the National Mission which slowly emerged from it dragged on without obvious success, or only with the kind of success which was suggested in the comment that a large number of Pharisees were going to church to express fervent regret at the sins of all the publicans. One can follow Temple's own developing attitudes through his editorship of *Challenge*, an Anglican weekly paper which was looking for a wider constituency than either the Evangelical or Anglo-Catholic parties, and through which Temple was widening his life-long search for a solid body of Anglican support for his political theology. *Challenge* asserted (30 July 1915) that there were still far too many people who had not yet realised 'how much we need purging for the work which shall, please God, be ours after the war'. This was largely a matter of middle-class purgation: there was no illusion about the difficulties faced by any attempt to extend the Mission to the working classes, though in June 1916 an editorial suggested that the National Mission hoped to save England from class-war. Even middle-class repentance, however, did not come easily, and in January 1916, the paper was complaining that the church had issued forms of public intercession which were stronger on Germany's sin than Britain's.

As the war continued *Challenge* began to link repentance for the past to a commitment to social change in the future, along the lines which Temple himself laid down in 1917 in *Mens Creatrix*. Even so, Temple's paper could not avoid ambiguity about the trade unions. The miners, especially, were regarded as a race apart: in the autumn of 1915, when conscription was already being discussed as the answer to the war's expanding demand for troops, the miners' leader, Smillie, had told the Union Conference that no class had a right to conscript another until the land and capital of the country was conscripted; the railwaymen opposed the idea on the same grounds. Conscription was an example of Temple's anxiety to be fair to the trade unions. *Challenge* defended the idea of conscription in a sentence characteristic of Temple's early political philosophy – 'it is simply the organizing of the general will' – but went on to assert that although the working classes felt themselves to be British subjects, they did not identify with Britain. They did not think of conscription as 'an organisation of themselves by themselves', but as coercion by a partly alien authority. This amounted to an admission that the 'general will' could not be invoked successfully just because the nation-state existed: a general will had to be created, and as far as the unions were concerned an appeal to patriotism was not enough to stimulate enthusiasm for conscription. What was needed, Challenge said, was a 'fellowship' (a theological expression which in this case meant cooperation between management and workforce) in time of danger which we had not sought in time of peace. This attempt to interpret the ideas of Labour brought complaints of 'Socialism' (26 November 1915). Characteristic, perhaps, of clerical opinion in the Church of England was the complaint of Winnington-Ingram, Anglicanism's chief recruiting-sergeant, that in the National Mission he had 'so far failed to meet the representatives of Labour' (12 May 1916).

In the summer and autumn of 1916, when Temple seems to have shared a widespread hope that a new offensive on the Western Front would prove decisive and bring the war to an end, this social anxiety, which was to flow into Life and Liberty, mounted quickly. The paper declared that after the war the unionised workers would not be happy at having to return to lower-paid work. There were also the unorganized and unskilled workers, who were the great majority, the thought of whom alarmed Challenge so much that one of the more desperate of Victorian solutions to the problem of poverty – 'a land settlement' – was revived quite seriously. In September 1916, when confidence of swift victory reached a new height, the paper ran an editorial on 'Demobilisation' which was concerned entirely with what should happen to the working classes after the war had ended. At the moment, the leader said, industry was private and its direction dictatorial, but in future Labour, which in all European countries would want a larger share in control of national policy, 'must be given its full place in the management of industry'. The point was repeated in the following week's editorial, this time on 'Trade Unionism'. By the end of the month anxiety was being expressed about the possibility of railway strikes, but this was balanced by the reminder that the workers involved really were deprived. As in the discussion of conscription, the editorial emphasis was on the need to form an actual nation out of divided classes.

As part of its campaign to move the National Mission in this direction *Challenge* underlined, late in 1916, under the heading 'Prophets and Priests', the difference between two views of the kind of repentance it was meant to promote. The paper supported those who wanted to concentrate on the great moral issues of the time such as international peace and industrial cooperation, 'claiming for the rule of Christ provinces which have as yet hardly been subject to it'. There were others, however, a more priestly element, 'which tends to be frightened by the extensions into political, civil and industrial life which the other party is endeavouring to secure' (20 October 1916). The bishops were included among the timid in a leader entitled 'Our Lack of Guidance' (3 November 1916) which demanded to know 'what lead has the Church received from the united Episcopate on the temperance question, on the question of the living wage, or the problem of housing, or the right use of capital, or the problems of Church Reform?' The Archbishop of Canterbury, Randall Davidson, was deeply offended by this kind of criticism, which did less than justice to his own support for 'spiritual independence' and which wildly exaggerated the practical possibility of 'temperance reform' (which really meant teetotalism) in the middle of a desperate war.

This persistent attempt to identify the Church of England with some radical, and some less than radical, social language was bound to make more conservative Anglicans feel that the less autonomy the Church of England had the better, because pressure for an official attitude in some of these areas was more likely to divide the church than to unify the nation. E. R. Norman (1976) has suggested that Temple suffered from a 'guilty moralism' which had affected upper-class Anglican theologians since the 1860s and which left him happier striking attitudes of class repentance than in proposing practical solutions. Norman quoted with approval a criticism of Temple which Charles Raven made in the 1920s, that 'some of my friends, not least the Bishop of Manchester [Temple] are very fond of talking about industrial problems as if all you had to do was to speak of them as vocation, and the whole spirit in which they were undertaken was changed' (Norman, 1976, p. 282).

It is not difficult to find editorials in *Challenge* which give grounds for such criticism, saying, for example, that the priesthood was not the only 'vocation', that 'our circumstances are planned by divine providence', that we should enter secular work 'with a full sense of vocation' (5 May 1916). Temple certainly suffered from the habitual preacher's temptation to soar above mere practicality, and even in 1916 he could hardly be expected to foresee just how unkind the twentieth century would be to the doctrine of providence. Nevertheless 'guilty moralism' exaggerates the case against him. The political organisation of the working classes had improved considerably since 1900, and the war inevitably gave the major unions more freedom of manoeuvre. There was nothing farfetched in 1916 about the

statement that all over Europe after the war 'Labour', as it was
still usually called, would expect more political power:
broadly speaking, this was what happened in the 1920s.
What Temple did not realise was how bitterly Labour's
expectations would be resisted: his naivety, which he shared
with many others, lay in the assumption that the defenders of
the status quo were irreversibly weaker than the unions and
the left-wing political parties. In England, a Conservative–
Liberal hegemony seemed to Temple to be coming to an end,
and he could be seen as pleading with his own church, at that
point still the dominant ecclesiastical body in the country, to
accept a larger share for the laity in the government of the
Church of England, and for the unions in the running of
industry and politics. This was not necessarily a guilt-ridden
attempt to impose a left-of-centre political solution on the
country as a whole, but rather a warning that the Church of
England might finally cut itself off from the working classes if
it simply acquiesced in the political imposition of a right-of-
centre solution, and profited from the confusion to keep the
laity in the church in a subordinate position. In the light of
what happened Temple's advice does not look so naive. 'The
divine life of the Church is in the whole Body', *Challenge* said
in June 1916, 'and only if the whole Body is active can the
vital power be complete.' The view that the laity should be
allowed to share in decisions about doctrine and ethics was
hardly radical. It was the doctrine of the church which John
Henry Newman had urged on the Vatican in vain in the
1860s, especially in his essay 'On Consulting the Faithful in
Matters of Doctrine', though Newman, who was too wise in
the ways of the Roman Curia to imagine that any concession
would be made, had been thinking about consulting small
groups of well-educated laymen over very long periods of
time. Temple, moved by his experiences in the Workers'
Educational Association, was worried about the lack of

contact between the state church and the working classes, and was aware, as were other Anglican clergymen, that the Church of England might like to think of itself as the church of the English people, but that it was not exactly the church of ordinary English people in post-Victorian urban society.

Another current of radical thought which passed through *Challenge* in 1916 and which would affect Life and Liberty from its inauguration in 1917 was dissatisfaction with the financial style of the establishment. These criticisms combined the demand for efficiency, which had been heard ever since the 1830s, with a call for simpler, more spontaneous ecclesiastical institutions. In February 1916, for example, *Challenge* declared that episcopal incomes should be reformed, and that episcopal palaces should be put to new uses. An unofficial committee was proposed to consider these matters, though at the end of July it was noted that no such committee had actually been set up. There was a constant assertion that the bishops lacked courage and were failing to lead. The tone, however, was never democratic, that is, the campaign for Anglican self-government and spiritual independence did not, at least as far as Temple was concerned, talk in terms of 'power to the laity', or even 'power to the presbyters', but accepted that the bishops should organise themselves to run the church as long as the church was run efficiently. The bishops were not meant to be 'ecclesiastical policemen', appointed to keep the warring Anglican liturgical clans in order, but should work in terms of a vision of the Church of England as a family which needed a common mind. There was no doubt about what the common mind ought to be thinking: 'there is in the Church a new thought about sin; a realisation of corporate sin and of personal responsibility for it . . . if there is to be a redemption of man there has to be a redemption of society' (*Challenge*, 17 December 1916). This was to be Temple's recurrent public programme: he believed that the Church of England should be free to take its own decisions, that in what he saw as a 'modern world' some kind of central representative body had to be set up to bring the priesthood and the laity into closer contact; he sympathised with the wartime reaction of some younger clergy against the establishment as pompously, snobbishly and expensively irrelevant; but all this was much less important than that the bishops should take Anglicanism in hand and set it on the proper path of transforming social attitudes to wealth and poverty.

A good example of this affection for the hierarchical may be found in Harry Blackburne, a distinguished chaplain on the Western Front and a supporter of Life and Liberty, who nevertheless wrote to his wife from Valenciennes with the British Army in 1919 that very little interest was being taken in the General Election at home, and added: 'I hope that the Coalition gets in with a big majority, for I do not think that democracy is yet safe for the world, even though the world is safe for democracy' (Blackburne, 1932, p. 183). Another product of the Army and a Dean of Clare College, Cambridge, P. C. T. Crick, argued that just as there were Labour and Conservative groups on most borough councils, 'it should be equally normal to find on every public body men who stand not for any shade of political opinion, but for the principles of social justice . . . the writer would contemplate with satisfaction even the definite formation in the country and in the House of Commons of something in the nature of a Christian Social party' (Crick, 1921, pp. 72–3). Crick was about to become a bishop in Australia and had written his impressions down about two years before. A comparison with Europe is relevant, because the Catholic Centre Party had existed in Germany since the Bismarckian unification, and in Italy the Partito Popolare Italiano had been founded by Catholic laymen in 1919 with papal acquiescence: by 1926,

Pius XI preferred to back Mussolini, who closed the Catholic Party down; it would reappear as the Christian Democratic Party in 1942.

In England the Anglican reformers continued to nibble at the establishment: in August 1916 *Challenge* applauded the Council of the National Mission for passing a resolution which criticised the Anglican systems of emoluments, endowments and patronage. The Council said that these practices were not in accordance with the spirit and teaching of Christ, were a serious stumbling-block in the way of many who were alienated from the church, were causing increasing misgiving among faithful members of the Church of England, and were impairing the efficiency of its work. Yet another committee of enquiry was demanded. It is interesting that at the beginning of the century the ill-starred Roman Catholic Modernists had shown a similar enthusiasm for a church which would depend less on social prestige and the appearance of political power. There is evidence in the pages of *Challenge* itself that the Modernist example was influencing the Anglican reformers.

Counter-currents also became apparent, for in November 1916 an editorial conceded that a bishop should have 'sufficiently commodious a house' to be hospitable, a withdrawal which was balanced by appealing to an idea which had been popular in the urban Settlement movement of the 1880s, that educated people should choose to live among the poor in the style of the poor, in order, as it was sometimes said, that culture might be transmitted by contact. This was clutching at straws rather than admitting to a sense of guilt, though guilt, in E. R. Norman's sense, had certainly been at work in the Victorian Settlements. *Challenge*'s uncertainty about bishops reflected the mood of a nation in difficulty and looking for leadership.

Lloyd George's new and allegedly more 'efficient' ministry

took power in December 1916, but by the spring of the next year Russia was falling apart and the United States was entering the war. The swirl of events beyond the shores of England and visibly out of English control also helped to unsettle the Church of England, for so long locked into Britain as the centre of the universe. Life and Liberty was a natural response. The idea of an Anglican reform pressure-group came from Dick Sheppard, a friend of Temple's who was Vicar of St Martin-in-the-Fields in West London from 1914 to 1926. Sheppard had vague ideas about quickening the religious life of the Church of England, but those whom he brought together concluded that the establishment had to be made more workable before it could become more religious, and committed themselves to 'vehement and violent' support for the proposals of the Selborne Report. Temple, who parted company with Sheppard in the 1930s when the latter, now a passionate pacifist, organised the ephemeral success of the Peace Pledge Union, wrote rather patronisingly about him after his death that 'if we think rather of the Movement (Life and Liberty) itself than of its goal, then he, far more than anyone else, *was* the Movement' (Roberts, 1942, p. 119). There was more to it than that, however. Iremonger, in his official biography of Temple, emphasised the gap which existed in Life and Liberty between those like Temple, for whom the conservative Selborne proposals were enough as a clearing of the ground, and those who really wanted disestablishment, 'because no freedom worth having could be gained without paying the highest price, and only a disestablished church could be truly and entirely free' (Iremonger, 1948, p. 223). This was Iremonger's own opinion, and he went on, at a distance of more than twenty years, to talk as though the early days of Life and Liberty had been like the French Revolution without the guillotine.

There is little substance in this vision of a revolution which

Temple betrayed, though for some of those involved, Life and Liberty became an alternative to the war going on in Europe, on the ground that the sacrifices of the soldiers could only be justified if the Church of England, at least symbolically, abandoned its traditional role as the religious face of the political system, and became a people's Anglicanism with a Franciscan style. Temple interpreted the goals of Life and Liberty differently: he wanted a national religious movement which would seek social goals so broad as to become political without becoming a political party. He saw Life and Liberty as the chance to form a pressure-group which could make a revitalised establishment an effective influence on social development. He wanted to diffuse a civic religion which would enable the establishment to go beyond the limits of the individual's personal life (which was the primary territory of the Life and Liberty radicals, whether Anglican Evangelical or Anglo-Catholic) and add to religious education new spheres of public influence in fields like industry, housing and health.

The most serious recent discussion of Life and Liberty is in Kenneth Thompson's *Bureaucracy and Church Reform* (1970). Thompson suggests that Temple played a major role in holding together a coalition of extremes. This is an exaggeration, because when a decision had to be taken as to how the proposed new House of Laity should be elected, Temple finally supported the proposal for a baptismal rather than a confirmation franchise, and so drove Gore effectively out of Anglican politics. The loss of Gore explained much which Iremonger lamented, but Temple, as one can see if one examines *Mens Creatrix*, which was published in 1917, was bound to favour an inclusive against an exclusive voting qualification, because he desired a truly national establishment, membership of which would, theologically, be conferred through baptism.

Temple seems to have been the better interpreter of the Church of England as it existed at the time. Neither Gore, who already wanted disestablishment in 1917, nor Henson, whose reaction against Life and Liberty logically led him to advocate disestablishment in the late 1920s, understood how deeply the ordinary Anglican adhered to the state connexion as defining Anglicanism socially, culturally, politically and religiously. The advocates of 'spiritual independence' played this down and wrote sentimental essays about 'Anglicanism' as tradition, as charm, as the quintessence of village England, as comprehensiveness, as the one major Christian institution which practised toleration even if not all its internal factions preached it. Temple could do this himself on occasion: for example, in an essay on 'The Genius of the Church of England' (1928) he could write that 'the Anglican note is "You may" in contrast with the Roman "You must", but the liberty so offered is a liberty to claim all the traditional privileges of the Catholic Church' (Temple, 1958, p. 94). Ordinary Anglicans, however, did not respond to such eulogies if they pointed away from establishment: they valued the connexion with the state and did not want to relinquish it. There was no majority in favour of going into the wilderness.

Nor did Temple manipulate or outwit the Archbishop of Canterbury. Davidson and his friends simply negotiated the best terms that they could get in Whitehall for the episcopate, that is, for the continuance of government from above. The Church Assembly which resulted was not democratic: there was no question of a single, elected body, and the House of Bishops was not elected at all. Thus there was no institutional surrender to the 'modern', if this meant 'democracy'. It was modernisation as efficiency which underwrote what changes there were: hence the quiet disappearance of Life and Liberty schemes for building in working-class representation. That the Enabling Act (1919) actually built in middle-class domination of the new House of Laity seemed perfectly in order to Davidson and his principal legal adviser, Sir Lewis Dibdin. It was true that during the World War anxiety (in which Temple shared) about the political and social power of working-class institutions had increased, more especially after the Russian Revolution in 1917. There was no wide enthusiasm, however, for giving working-class people more influence in the Church of England. Temple's personal connexions with the WEA led nowhere, because the political leaders of the working classes did not for a moment suppose that radical Anglican reform was likely. And indeed, we are still discussing the proportion of 'public-school men' among the bishops in the 1990s.

Despite its good intentions, Life and Liberty reflected a complacent feeling that educated Christians had only to exert themselves to cross a communication gap, and the working classes would cheerfully embrace Christianity. The Army chaplains encouraged the view that the mass of ordinary soldiers were ignorant about religion; they did not suspect that late Victorian working-class culture had understood what the Christian churches taught and had rejected it, partly on the ground that the moral teaching of the church was against progress for the poor (as the ninth, disregarded appendix of the Selborne Report put it and as Temple and Mansbridge were well aware) and partly on the ground that the Christian dogmatic system was obsolete. Anglican intellectuals like Temple thought that they could persuade the churches to support the social and political advance of the working classes, and so conciliate them, but they paid little attention to the dogmatic issues, preferring to attribute the existence of a critical attitude towards Christianity to 'the materialistic education of the people since 1870: the board schools are good, but the outlook of the 70s and 80s was grossly materialistic, and the present men and women were educated then' (Selborne, 1917, p. 253). Nevertheless, the same report went on, with characteristic religious optimism, materialism was on the wane and 'the sentiment of the majority of the average workers is curiously favourable to the necessity for some authoritative rule of life'. It was taken for granted that if the working classes were full of 'a deep religious idealism' (p. 250), then all that was needed was a clear statement of the main lines of Christian theology. In Temple's mind, this argument led back to the overwhelming importance of religious education in schools. Selborne failed to distinguish between 'religion' and 'Christianity': these discussions constantly assumed that to be religious was to be Christian, and that not to be Christian was not to be religious: that some working-class people might have *religious* assumptions which differed from those of the Anglican sub-culture was not often suspected.

Life and Liberty was launched at a meeting in the Queen's Hall, London, on 16 July 1917. The movement had been announced in a letter to *The Times* (20 June 1917), signed by Temple as 'chairman' and by Iremonger and Sheppard as secretaries. Other significant signatories were A. A. David, the Headmaster of Rugby, J. B. Seaton, Principal of Cuddesdon Theological College, A. L. Smith, Master of Balliol, Albert Mansbridge of the WEA and Louise Creighton. This letter said that the only way to reform the church's 'antiquated machinery' was to alter the procedure for putting church legislation through the House of Commons, and that the Selborne Report offered a viable way of doing this. 'If the Church is to have new life, even if it is to maintain the life which is has, it must have liberty', the letter continued, 'even at the cost, if necessary, of disestablishment . . . We believe that the leaders of the Church are ready to advance along the path of progress if they are assured of an earnest and widespread desire to go forward. But with or without them we are constrained by love of our Church and country to raise the standard of advance.'

The reference to disestablishment was described by Iremonger, in his biography of Temple, as unheroic, a sop to the radicals, but it already went much further than Temple had seemed to be going when he contacted Davidson in February 1917. Then he almost apologised for the existence of Dick Sheppard's 'group', which (he said) had been brought to boiling point by the war and the National Mission; he argued that if he and others like him joined Sheppard, they would prevent the group from becoming more dissentient. As a rising but junior parish priest Temple could hardly have launched Life and Liberty without some reference to the Archbishop, who when he replied cautiously declined to comment on ecclesiastical 'Forward Movements'. He was in favour of 'spiritual independence' as long as he controlled the direction which it took, but had no desire to end the state connexion, and must have welcomed Henson's letter to The Times denouncing the appearance of Life and Liberty as 'a movement for Disestablishment from within', and saying that at most there might be a Royal Commission on the subject when the war was over.

Temple replied to Henson (The Times, 28 June 1917), and according to Iremonger had no difficulty in rebutting his criticism, but Iremonger did not quote the most dramatic section of the answer in which Temple deliberately said that 'our movement is not aiming at Disestablishment; it aims at self-government for the Church. Many of us, including myself, would infinitely prefer to secure that end by some other means than Disestablishment . . . But we feel the need of self-government to be so vital that we are prepared to face even Disestablishment if self-government can be obtained in no other way.' In view of this letter one can hardly agree with

Kenneth Thompson that Davidson would have been surprised by the resolution passed at the Queen's Hall Life and
Liberty meeting in July. Temple had in any case sent Davidson
an advance copy of what he was going to say at the Queen's
Hall.

The resolution said that Life and Liberty should approach
the Archbishops to urge them to find out 'whether and on
what terms Parliament is prepared to give freedom to the
Church in the sense of full power to manage its own life'. The
pressure was maintained when *Challenge* reported (27 July
1917) that at the launch-meeting 'expressions of belief in the
Establishment were received with respect but without
enthusiasm: expressions of the determination of the Life and
Liberty Council to face even disestablishment for the sake of
liberty at once called forth applause'. There had been support
from *The Times* (7 July 1917), which said, no doubt with a
certain ambiguity, that 'a democratic age demands government on the widest possible basis'.

Although the Queen's Hall meeting thoroughly established Temple's reputation as a leader, what happened is
usually seen through the jaundiced mind of Henson. This
bias goes back to George Bell's biography of Randall
Davidson (1935), where Bell left the impression that
Henson's contemptuous dismissal of the meeting in a private
letter to the Archbishop (17 July 1917) was reliable. Bell had
been a devoted chaplain to Davidson from 1914 to 1924, and
he may have used Henson's letter as a way of defending the
Archbishop's hostility towards the Life and Liberty movement. Henson, whose letter is described by E. R. Norman
(1976, p. 275) as 'withering, well-known and completely
accurate', attacked the composition of the meeting:

The audience was three parts composed of women, and the
remaining part was made up of youngish parsons. Socially, I
conjecture that the meeting consisted of upper middle-class

people, who form the congregations of West-end churches. There was no trace of the working classes perceptible ... The Headmasters seem to be deep in the movement. David of Rugby read prayers and the Headmasters of Eton and Harrow were on the platform ... The academic, the feminist, the socialist, the clericalist [Anglo-Catholic] ... these are not the constituents of an ecclesiastical policy which is likely to be tolerant, or virile, or just, or large.

Henson denied that the meeting had been enthusiastic, characteristically suggesting that this was partly because of 'the great predominance of women', and he ridiculed the younger speakers: 'A returned chaplain in khaki [this was Harry Blackburne, who had served in France since 1914] assured us that great numbers of officers and men were eagerly longing for the prompt and drastic handling of the Church: and Mr "Dick" Sheppard concluded with an ecstatic appeal for enthusiasm.' As for Maude Royden, being a woman, it is hardly surprising that Henson thought her 'confused, incoherent, and, when intelligible, irrelevant' (1942, pp. 207–8).

Henson was entitled to be angry about vague threats of disestablishment, and he was justified in some of his criticisms of what in his reminiscences he called 'Gore's crowd' – the Anglo-Catholics; but the letter expressed more than that. For all his display of anti-intellectualism he was himself an intellectual in the not unusual position of finding his views ignored by people whom he would have liked to influence: he would not always have been so critical of the Headmasters of Eton and Harrow. No doubt some of the active service chaplains behaved as though the end of the old world was at hand, an idea repulsive to Henson, but he showed no imaginative grasp of their experience. In his reminiscences, written twenty-five years later, he was still content to say that the war 'had brought to prominence a considerable number of the younger clergy, who had gained in the course of their military service a dislike of the restrictions imposed by normal ecclesiastical discipline . . . Why should the experimental licence of the camp be disallowed in the parish? Their zeal was great, their pastoral experience small [sic], their practical sagacity untested, and their popular favour high. They formed the backbone of the Life and Liberty movement' (1942, p. 206). This is poor stuff, as was his apology for the political tone of his opinions, that 'in 1917 the longing for peace threatened to become uncontrollable by reason and patriotism, and the triumph of Communism was giving a dangerous impetus to social and economic discontents in Britain' (p. 205). These discontents included feminism: here the symbolic offender, as far as Henson was concerned, was Maude Royden, who may or may not have spoken well on this occasion but whose real crimes lay elsewhere: not only was she a lay member of the Church of England who had preached and baptised at the Congregationalist City Temple in London, but she had joined the Fellowship of Reconciliation, a pacifist organisation founded in December 1914. In the previous year the National Mission had been bitterly torn apart by opposition to 'preaching' by Anglican women, and Temple was unable to prevent Anglo-Catholic intransigence driving her off the Life and Liberty Council in October 1917. Henson was not likely to admit that 'Gore's crowd' shared his view of women as, ecclesiastically, a servant class.

We should be cautious, therefore, in supposing that Henson's general view of the Church of England made him a reliable witness to Anglican reform movements. 'There was not much stuff', he complained, in Temple's address at the Queen's Hall. Yet on the question of church and state Temple tried to be constructive, saying that he believed that 'establishment counts for something as a national profession of faith, and may count for very much in this direction in the future. I believe that the connexion of Church and State tends to provide some hallowing sanction and restraint to the activities of the State . . . while it also gives the Church a vantage ground for preaching national righteousness.' He echoed the fear expressed by the Army chaplains that this was a moment at which the Church of England must not fail to act: this was why Parliament should be approached even though the war continued. Both Davidson and Henson saw this proposal as an attempt to snatch control of the church from the proper hands, and Henson must have writhed as Temple declared that 'the coming age will be increasingly democratic. We are fighting now for democracy against autocracy. No doubt if you identify Church and State you can say that if the State which controls ecclesiastical activities is democratic, all will be well. But no one, apart from a few theorists, believes in that identification in so complete a form. And if the Church is to be democratic, it must be through representation, councils or Synods possessed of real power to act . . . Only so can we be again the Church of the people.'

In a passionate peroration Temple appealed, as he always did when he was deeply moved (it was part of his deep religious conservatism) to the eschatological theme:

The day is come that burns like fire, for Christ has cast his fire upon the earth. Come out from your safety and comfort, come out from your habits and conventions. Listen for the voice of the wind as it sweeps over the world and stand where you may be caught in its onward rush. Not now in ecclesiastical debate; not now in the careful defence of established positions won long ago is the service of God's Kingdom to be rendered; but in the establishment of justice between nation and nation; between capital and labour, between men and women. Here is your task. Will you perform it? Or will you stay as you are, to flicker out, a lamp that gives no light, unmourned and even unnoticed? So the Spirit calls. And shall we be deaf to that call? We cannot heed it loyally and effectively unless we have such power of control over our own action as may enable us to become a united and compact striking force, knowing our goal and agreeing about the way to reach it. We can only be worthy of our name – the Body of Christ – strong to do his will and supple to adapt our action to the needs of our day, when we have freedom to act as the Spirit guides us. We claim liberty for the sake of life. (Davidson Papers, vol. 255)

Henson could not match this Edwardian oratory, nor for that matter did Temple himself often go so far – one is reminded of that passage at the close of *Mens Creatrix*, also published in 1917, in which he declared that without the doctrine of the Trinity 'the universe is completely unintelligible'. At the Queen's Hall, moreover, Temple's enthusiasm left the domestic aims of Life and Liberty far behind: a reformed, rejuvenated church would seek to establish justice between men and women, capital and labour, nation and nation. Such aims were inherently political, and Henson had no use for them. As his reminiscences make clear, he interpreted the problems of Anglicanism in the early twentieth century as a conflict between his 'Protestantism' and Gore's Anglo-Catholicism, whereas this essentially Victorian struggle was what Temple was trying to transcend. Henson had no conception of Temple's feelings about such questions as the relationship between Capital and Labour. In the context of the Queen's Hall meeting Temple sounded like a would-be national leader, and it is not surprising that Davidson sent him an acid letter on 17 July 1917 (Davidson Papers, vol. 255). He said:

I try to picture, if it were conceivable, someone reading that speech fifty years hence without any knowledge at all of what were the contemporary happenings in England. Would such a reader conjecture that there had been during the last year a National Mission inaugurated by the Archbishops 'off their own bat', and that the committees appointed as a result for the practical questions of the hour were now vigorously in session . . . On the contrary, I should have pictured Bishops of the order of Lucretian divinities, or say like the eighteenth-century Archbishops Cornwell or Moore, bewigged and besleeved, who might doubtless pass placid resolutions in Convocation but had no thought of putting them into action. I know this is not the sort of picture you meant to draw.

As Davidson suspected, this was the sort of picture which Temple wanted to imply. The National Mission had high-lighted the divisions inside the Church of England, and Davidson's appeal to 'committees' was far from a commit-ment to action. Temple's strong point was that the Selborne Report had already been published, that the bishops had welcomed it in May 1917, but gave no sign of doing anything about what it recommended. Davidson insisted that 'all men are absorbed in war thoughts', that it was impossible for him 'to insist on an interview at Downing Street, which generally means calling the Prime Minister out of a Cabinet meeting to speak standing up in the ante-room, and ask him what conditions of Church life he would regard as the right ones for the future'. One had to wait for 'the first moment that is really available in the political and national life' – clearly after the war. For Davidson there was no deep-seated crisis in the relations between church and state: for him that relationship was concentrated in his personal contacts as Archbishop with prominent politicians and members of the Royal Family. Professor Hastings notes his tireless lobbying and expresses surprise that he is not even mentioned in standard histories of England in the first half of the century (Hastings, 1986, p. 62). Davidson would also have been surprised at the omission, but his minor exercises in 'high politics' did not amount to a significant *Anglican* policy. The political limi-tations of his office were to be cruelly exposed both in the General Strike and in the Prayer Book controversy of 1927/8.

In a pamphlet, *Life and Liberty*, published in 1917, Temple had already emphasised the Archbishop's isolation and, using the analogy of wartime Britain, had suggested that the Archbishop needed either a War Cabinet or a General Staff.

Temple replied to Davidson's private criticism, assuring the Archbishop that he had not meant to satirise the bishops, but also making quite clear what he expected him to do: either move a resolution in the House of Lords or introduce a bill there, so as to force the issue. At the same time he and Sheppard were negotiating through Bell for a meeting between a Life and Liberty deputation and the two Archbishops, which finally took place on 1 August 1917. There was a deputation of twenty-five, including Iremonger and Temple; Duncan-Jones (later Dean of Chichester); C. F. Garbett (later Archbishop of York); Guy Rogers (an Evangelical, later Canon of Birmingham); A. E. J. Rawlinson (later Bishop of Derby); Francis Underhill (later Dean of Rochester); Douglas Eyre (Head of Oxford House, the Anglo-Catholic Settlement in London, where he had succeeded Iremonger, who had followed Sheppard); Albert Mansbridge and Lady Mary Trefusis. Eyre and Mansbridge, like Temple, had been members of the Selborne Committee.

At this meeting Temple's problem was that Life and Liberty had no simple way of leading the Church of England without the Archbishop, and no way at all of making the Archbishop lead Life and Liberty. Davidson listened to speeches from Temple, Garbett and Mansbridge, but said politely that he would do nothing until after the Representative Church Council, an unwieldy and unimportant body of clergy and laity numbering several hundred which had only been set up on a temporary footing in 1913, had met some time in November 1917 and given a view on the Selborne Report. Foxed for the moment, Temple wrote to the Archbishop (7 August 1917), saying that he and his wife had taken the

Manor Cottage at Ramsbury near Hungerford and would be delighted if Davidson and his wife would like to spend some time in the country with them. Davidson naturally declined this attempt to apply more personal pressure, and the Council of Life and Liberty decided to hold a retreat at Cuddesdon, the Anglo-Catholic seminary near Oxford, at the beginning of October. This gathering was marred by the insistence of Cuddesdon's principal, J. B. Seaton, that Maude Royden, as an Anglican woman who had baptised three Congregationalist children, could not be permitted to sleep at the seminary; Temple was helpless, and Maude Royden resigned from the Council. Iremonger (1948, pp. 236–8) excused Temple rather fulsomely and bewailed the collapse of a revolution, but this was not the point: the incident showed that now that change in the constitutional position of the Church of England seemed inevitable, the main church parties were moving to protect their own interests against the effects of change. Fundamentally, Life and Liberty had already lost the struggle to dictate what the battle was about.

Nevertheless, by 11 October 1917 Temple was able to send Davidson an outline of the Life and Liberty programme. The text, which could have evoked no sympathy in Davidson's mind, echoes the broad lines of the Queen's Hall speech and concentrated on what would now be called 'political theology'. 'The Church', it said, 'is commissioned to bring to bear upon all phases and problems of life, political, social and economic, no less than personal, the mind of Christ wherein alone is to be found the true basis of human life. The Church has in the past not given effective witness to the mind of Christ on such matters as international relations, industrial order, wealth and poverty and the like . . .' In other words, the Life and Liberty case for changing the structure of the establishment was not based on what Davidson and others meant when they talked about the need for 'spiritual independence', that is, freedom for the senior bishops to run the Church of England in their own quiet way, but on the quite different claim that the national church ought to be free and organised to change society as well as evangelise it. That Temple regarded this as the proper ground for action was made obvious by the further statement that the church 'is disqualified by abuses in its own administrative system from giving effective witness to the way of justice and love . . . When the Church sets itself to give its witness and to reform its own abuses it finds itself hampered by lack of means of corporate self-expression, and by restrictions which under present conditions it is powerless to alter.' It was on this basis that Life and Liberty claimed for the church 'liberty in the sense of full power to control its own life through representative and responsible assemblies'.

The programme also proposed amendments to the Selborne Report. One of these, that women should have the right to vote for and serve on all representative church bodies, including any central assembly, was a response to contemporary feeling and was finally accepted. Another, that the basic qualification for electors to the parochial parish councils should be baptism together with a declaration of membership in the Church of England, but that the elected representatives should also be communicants, reflected the division between Temple and Gore, who would have preferred an electorate restricted to communicants. On the basis of this programme Temple tried to persuade the Archbishop to give him a letter saying that he agreed with a basic statement that only in Christ could be found the true basis for civilisation, and that Davidson thought that the Church of England needed freedom of action. This attempt to involve Davidson in Life and Liberty – because Temple would then have used the letter in the national campaign which the movement was developing – was unsuccessful: Davidson was bound to feel that such an overtly political church could not possibly remain established for long.

Temple added to this request the information that Sheppard and Iremonger were pressing him to resign St James's, Piccadilly and lead the national campaign for Life and Liberty. Temple was thirty-six, had been married for about fifteen months, and had what was then a very comfortable living of more than £2,000 a year. He asked Davidson:

But do you consider that I can count on getting a post which would both give me work for the Church and enough to live on fairly soon after the conclusion of this special job? I would, of course, write to your Grace, and one or two Bishops, perhaps those who administer the Crown appointments, when I thought that the termination of my special job was about six months off. From the point of view of one's usefulness through life one is bound to consider such a point. And in all our circumstances we should be in a financially impossible position unless we can count on this. (Davidson Papers, vol. 255)

Davidson replied with a firm negative: 'I do not feel that I can appropriately write a letter to be read in Churches about your movement . . . it is not yet concrete enough in form . . .' (25 October 1917). He made no comment on Temple's plan to resign St James's, so that when Temple told him on 27 October that he had decided to give up St James's in the New Year, he added that 'I fear that you would have felt more cause for rejoicing if my decision had come the other way' (Davidson Papers, vol. 255).

One can exaggerate the personal risks that Temple was taking: it is noticeable, for example, that Gore, in approving the idea, added that he greatly wished Temple to be made a bishop, 'but on the whole I am disposed to think that that would not be affected'; nor was it, for Temple became a

Canon of Westminster in July 1919 and Bishop of Manchester in 1921. Iremonger saw Temple's departure from St James's as in part a criticism of the Anglican episcopate's cosy wartime existence, in line with the attacks which *Challenge* had made on bishops' incomes and palaces. Once again, and even more emphatically than in the past, Temple was putting himself forward as a national Anglican leader. His action was impressive because at a time when the clergy incessantly talked about other people's 'sacrifices' he was himself giving something up voluntarily. Whether, on the other hand, his gesture (and the hard work of itinerant propaganda which followed) made as much difference to the outcome as is usually assumed is more difficult to say. Iremonger, Sheppard and other extremists still hoped that Davidson could be made to act in wartime, but the plain fact is that nothing took place until the war was over, as Davidson had wanted, and the Enabling Act of 1919 conformed to his limited views.

In a letter written on 31 October 1917, Davidson made clear that he was not going to bless Temple's decision to become a full-time leader of Life and Liberty. Nevertheless, on 8 November 1917, Temple pleaded once more with the Archbishop to make a statement in favour of the Selborne Report, but again was firmly told by Bell that nothing would be done before the Representative Council met. When it did so, no vote was taken on the merits of the Selborne Report, but another committee was asked for, to consider what should be done. This provoked Temple and the Life and Liberty Council, which met on 4 December 1917 and issued an angry public statement (*The Times*, 7 December 1917) which criticised the Anglican bishops for not challenging the delaying tactics of the majority in the Representative Church Council, declared that the procedure adopted did not suggest urgency, and continued:

We have waited long enough. We have attempted to offend no one. To this end we have met together always to deliberate and never to act. We are weary of perpetual deliberation. A disturbance would be better than perpetual inactivity. Need we calculate much longer? We are clear that the Church just now has her greatest and possibly her last opportunity of vindicating her Catholic and national character. But this can only be achieved by a struggle fierce and sustained, by a purging thorough and sincere, and by a summons such as many had hoped might be issued during these days of war to dare anything, that the will of God might be done, as in Heaven, so on earth.

What Life and Liberty could achieve, huffing and puffing apart, was not obvious, but the talk about 'struggles' and 'purgings' and 'daring anything' all suggested a powerful desire, not least on Temple's own part, to find some sanctified equivalent of the war itself in this internal Anglican contest. He had written to Davidson on 4 December 1917 to warn him of what was about to be published; Davidson told Louise Creighton on the same day that Temple was 'rather apologetic in tone', and had claimed that he (Temple) had ensured that nothing violent or rude remained in the final version for which he was responsible. The Archbishop hit back immediately, saying that he thought that Mrs Creighton 'feels a little uncomfortable about the published letter', and that he was sure that other members of Life and Liberty were feeling the same. He asked how many people had voted for publication of the letter in the Life and Liberty Council (Temple replied on 10 December 1917, saying that there had been about thirty-one people at the meeting, and that there had been two dissentients). Davidson rejected any suggestion that Life and Liberty was helping him to solve the problem of church government, and insisted that the movement was mistaken in assuming that anything could be done at the parliamentary level 'at the present moment'. The style of his justification was characteristic:

I am mixing for hours on most days in the week with the men prominent in our public life on whose aid we should have to rely if the changes we want were to be made, and I do not literally know one of them who would share your view as to the practicability of the forward push in an official way at the present moment when every thought and every ounce of energy is absorbed in England's struggle for its very life. This makes me absolutely certain that I have been right in advocating or insisting upon the necessity of our eschewing a policy of hustle and push in matters ecclesiastical during these months of daily and nightly strain upon the thoughts and time of every public man who is worthy of the name. (Davidson Papers, vol. 256)

Davidson was determined to stay in control, and Temple could not shake him. He wrote again on 21 December 1917, trying to persuade the Archbishop to underwrite the Life and Liberty crusade which he was now beginning in his full-time position. In 1918 he spoke in city after city, including Birmingham, Bradford, Cambridge, Grimsby, Huddersfield, Liverpool, Walsall and Great Yarmouth. 'There is a sense hard to dispel', he said, 'even by quoting your own words, that in desiring self-government for the Church we are raising a standard of revolt against the Church authorities.' Davidson was immovable. He did not mind if Temple wanted to educate Anglicans in the need for a livelier church, but an archiepiscopal proclamation 'would serve as an irritant rather than an encouragement to a vast number of good laymen who would think that they are being dragooned or bullied into an opinion whereto they may quite amenably be led' (28 December 1917). He was too wise to raise any objection to Temple's becoming a member of the committee appointed by the Representative Church Council to draft proposals for constitutional change, only observing that 'if he cannot come to the same conclusion as the Committee does, so be it, and he must act as seems to him right' (11 January 1918, to the Clerk of the Council).

Only when it was certain that Temple had abandoned St James's, Piccadilly and had launched his full-time campaign did Davidson carefully make sure that his communications were still open with the radical. He apologised, for what it was worth, for not having advised Temple about leaving or not leaving St James's. He admitted that he had been chary of saying anything which could be taken as meaning that 'the call of duty for you was the giving up of St James's. I could not satisfy myself on that point . . . Now, however, that the Rubicon is crossed, and you are in harness for the great enterprise of teaching the Church the full meaning of life and liberty, I have no qualms about wishing you, with all my heart, God speed' (26 January 1918, Davidson Papers, vol. 256). Iremonger called this 'the letter which [Temple] has longed for', and said that his gratitude for it 'lost no degree of its warmth in the strenuous controversy that followed' (Iremonger, 1948, pp. 250−1). It is true that Temple was far too good a diplomat to allow himself to quarrel with the Archbishop, but this letter, though friendly, still gave him no room to identify Davidson with his national mission.

The time-table was Davidson's. In 1918 the committee appointed by the Representative Church Council slowly worked out its views on the Selborne Report. By June 1918 Temple was again telling the Archbishop that Life and Liberty wanted parliamentary action as soon as possible, without waiting for the end of the war. By then, however, the point was already lost. The report of the Representative Church Council appeared on 3 October 1918, and on 11 October Temple asked Davidson to receive what was originally to be a small deputation from Life and Liberty, the Church Self-Government Association, 'and possibly other societies'.

Davidson agreed to a meeting on 24 October 1918. Iremonger took over the details, and again asked (on October 17) for a public statement committing the Archbishops to the aims of Life and Liberty: Davidson declined. In a second letter (23 October 1918) Iremonger admitted that the deputation would actually consist of about eighty people, but that although the Church League for Women's Suffrage would be represented, he and Temple did not propose to raise the question of the position of women in the church: the women were included in the deputation because they were in favour of Anglican self-government. The deputation came and went, and Davidson then wrote to The Times (5 December 1918) saying that what the Representative Church Council said was 'sound in principle'. In this way Davidson not only avoided any endorsement of the various 'movements', but also sidelined those who, like Hensley Henson (now Bishop of Hereford), wanted to organise public opposition to any change. Reform came 'from above': the Representative Church Council met in February 1919, and proposed a scheme which was adopted almost unanimously by the Convocations in May 1919, and an enabling bill, which gave legal substance to the Church Assembly, passed through Parliament without sustained opposition.

One way of summing up this discussion is to look at a typical article which Temple wrote in defence of the final proposals. It appeared in the Spectator (31 May 1919) as a reply to four critical articles by J. St Loe Strachey, who feared that the Church of England might cease to be 'the nation on its spiritual side' and become simply an episcopal denomination. Temple's reply was not as ardent as one might have expected. He was beginning to see what had actually been achieved as compared with the Life and Liberty programme. There was no danger of 'unchurching the nation', he said, because Parliament would keep its full control. There was no fear that measures distasteful to 'the nation' would slip through, 'for if they are distasteful to the nation they will certainly be distasteful also to a large part of the Church . . . Parliament will have very full warning that it needs to be vigilant.' The argument was confident, but Temple was admitting that the Church of England was not achieving full self-government or becoming spiritually independent. This was more true than he realised in 1919, because when Davidson's reforms and the brand of Westminster management on which he counted when he supported change were tested in 1927/8, the House of Commons listened to 'the nation' rather than to Davidson and the Church Assembly.

There was a second important point on which later critics came down on the same side as Strachey. He had presciently argued that in practice the Church Assembly would become sectarian because its benches would be filled with 'ecclesiastically-minded laymen' and not ordinary Anglicans. Temple knew that Life and Liberty had lost the battle to guarantee that at least the WEA would be indirectly represented in the Church Assembly, and he also knew that Life and Liberty itself was now being supported by Anglican laymen who thought that a reformed Church of England would be a useful barrier to social change. He tried to weaken Strachey's argument by asking why it was worse for a churchman to be ecclesiastically minded than for a citizen to be politically minded; he optimistically denied that the 'average Churchman' was going to sit idly by while some small clique effectively ran the establishment. It was not a small clique that Strachey had in mind, however, but a large one, and one which did not support Temple's wider programme. At the close of his article he sounded his own Life and Liberty note again, saying that the purpose of the Enabling Act was that the church might be able to reform itself and become 'a corporate living witness to the principles of the Kingdom of

God before the world and if necessary against the world. It is the giving of such witness which constitutes its life as a Church; it is the acceptance of such witness which can alone deliver the world from its distress.'

For the moment Temple had failed. The Church Assembly would not, in the 1920s, reflect his anxieties about the broader issue of the establishment's relationship to state and society. He would try again by organising Copec and the Birmingham Conference of 1924. Davidson, unintentionally aided by Henson, had succeeded in confining debate to a narrow discussion of 'disestablishment', which has never become a serious issue, and the problem of church legislation, which was genuine but trivial. Temple's much wider vision of the role of the English church in modern society stirred the imagination of only a few.

## THE ECUMENICAL MOVEMENT

Temple's role in the early stages of the Ecumenical Movement has been indicated in the first chapter. Between 1918 and the mid 1930s the Movement continued without making any important progress towards church unity. There were two major forms of procedure, one through a Committee of Faith and Order, which organised discussion on the strongly held disagreements which surrounded such subjects as the doctrines of the church and the priesthood; and the other through the Life and Work Committee, which in theory dealt with the practical problem of applying Christian principles in national and international life. The two groups overlapped, and the Life and Work slogan, 'doctrine divides but service unites', already expressed a certain antagonism between them. Moreover, from the first major Life and Work Conference, which took place in Stockholm in 1925, there was already present another division, between the 'social gospel' tendency to believe that a 'Kingdom of God' could be achieved through human effort, and the opposing view, popular in Germany but also championed by the American theologian, Reinhold Niebuhr, that the 'Kingdom' came only at the divinely ordained climax of human history. Faith and Order, meanwhile, whose first international conference was held at Lausanne in 1927, had fallen under the domination of A. C. Headlam, the crabbedly conservative Bishop of Gloucester, who opposed any scheme which would put an end to Faith and Order's separate existence. In the mean time the global family of Protestant churches were as far off union as ever.

It is evident that by the middle 1930s Temple had decided to work for a new solution. The World Council of Churches which was now proposed was not so much a step towards complete unity, as a device which would enable the Protestant churches to draw attention to their view of the rapidly worsening economic and political crisis. Around Temple was a small group of religious professionals, most of whom had learned their attitudes and methods in the Student Christian Movement before 1914. They spent their lives trying to organise an efficient international network of Protestant activity: they formed a spiritual but also political bureaucracy whose centre was not the restricted ethos of their national churches. J. H. Oldham, William Paton, John Mott, Marc Boegner and George Bell were members of this group, with Temple himself as acknowledged leader. Oldham, Paton and Temple all habitually thought in an imperial context.

What they wanted was a permanent body, the later 'World Council', which could represent all the major Christian groups which lay outside the Roman Catholic Church. In the long run they intended to include the missionary societies, which were already related in the International Missionary

Council. This did not mean a single, united church, but an institution which would have roots in the churches and which could operate as though the major Protestant and Orthodox churches, despite their disunity, had agreed to become a pressure-group. Such a plan was bound to be resisted by those people in the ecumenical movement, not least in Faith and Order, who feared the creation of a 'superchurch': Faith and Order had always been a theological debating society whose discussions committed nobody and were not leading towards a reunited 'church'.

An important element in the background of this plan for a 'council' was the postwar idealism which had gone into the foundation of the League of the Nations, an institution which had been conceived as a supranational body which would be able to revise the Versailles peace treaty where this proved to be necessary, and which would solve the problems of impending conflict between member nations, no one actually knew how. As far back as 1925 the Stockholm Conference of Life and Work had called for the churches to give the League of Nations a 'Christian soul', but this made little sense if the churches had no equivalent of the League through which to apply this spiritual pressure. By 1937 the political situation had darkened so much that it was possible for the Oxford Life and Work Conference to be told that the League was 'a ghostly shadow of what it was hoped it might become': Visser't Hooft, who became the first secretary of the proposed World Council when he was thirty-seven, largely on Temple's insistence, recalls in his Memoirs (1973) that Lord Robert Cecil, one of the most stubborn of the League's defenders, continued to insist at the Oxford Conference that 'in spite of recent events the level of international morality is higher than it was', and that the churches should still advocate support for the League (p. 72). In religious circles the cult of the League became a convenient substitute for an ecclesiastical critique of foreign policy. One could not say that it was also a convenient way of avoiding the alternative of religious pacifism, because, as we shall see, pacifism was openly and bitterly debated.

At the Oxford Conference, Life and Work pushed ahead with the plan for a 'World Council of Churches', and Temple temporarily solved the problem of its authority in 1938 by declaring that the officers and resolutions of the proposed World Council would not be able to bind member churches, and that the authority of any statements made would depend on their content: in other words, no 'superchurch' would limit the sovereignty of the member churches. Temple, Oldham and Paton were satisfied with this kind of machinery because they were accustomed to working on politicians through personal contacts, and to setting up small ad hoc committees to analyse specific problems; their experience predated the arrival of media politics, when influence has often to be exercised by a public manipulation of uninformed emotions.

At the time, Temple's definition of the power of the new body was sufficient to maintain ecumenical momentum at a time when the 'Council' did not yet exist, so that no actual conflict of power could take place; but when the same explanation – that there was no question of the World Council being or becoming a superchurch – was reaffirmed in a different postwar world by the Toronto Declaration of 1952, it was a sign that the heart had gone out of the effort to create a powerful new centre of international Christian opinion. In the mid 1930s Temple and his associates were agreed that such a body was needed to act and speak on behalf of the non-Roman churches in the way that the International Missionary Council was able to negotiate with governments on behalf of missionaries. The Oxford Life and Work Conference (1937) had a strong sense of the church being under attack; no one wanted a Protestant Vatican, but there was an awareness that separate denominations were at a disadvantage in dealing with the outside world compared with the Church of Rome.

This process is usually traced back to the Edinburgh World Missionary Conference in 1910, but it would be truer to say that the plans for a 'World Council' were thought of as a response to a specific, changed situation. At Oxford in 1937 Life and Work formally acknowledged the need for what was called a symbolic presentation of the unity of all Christians in face of unchristian and anti-Christian tendencies in the modern world. There was no evidence that such a unity existed except at an abstract level, but the ideological attacks on the churches and the physical persecution of German Protestants by the Nazis, which had intensified since 1934, combined with the feeling that ethically the churches were being by-passed by socialism, made the ecumenical leaders feel that they had suddenly drifted into a hostile world very unlike what most of them had known in their youth. When they considered international power-politics, many of them were influenced by the belief that the national churches had often weakened their position in Western society by their attitudes during the 1914–18 war. They saw in Spain in the late 1930s the spectacle of a local church being forced to choose directly between the Republicans and General Franco. They wanted to assert the existence of a Christian opinion which was more than national. Looked at in this light, the process of forming the World Council may be seen as primarily a Protestant defensive operation, intended to show that 'the church' was performing a proper, significant role in a continuing world crisis.

Temple was not entirely innocent in this failure, because the test case, which was whether or not the World Council could take a definite stand on the political issues of the Second

World War, was decided negatively while he was still alive and leader of the Provisional Committee. There was the problem, which Temple emphasised, that throughout these years the Council was still provisional, that there was no clear membership and no finally accepted constitution, and that the Council therefore lacked authority, but this was not the underlying reason for the Council's silence. Prominent clerics willingly made their own public statements about the war, but could not agree on a common statement which would claim to express the 'mind' of the church.

Already, in April 1939, when Hitler had torn up the Munich agreement by entering what was left of Czechoslovakia, the Swiss Protestant theologian Karl Barth had told Visser't Hooft, the secretary of the World Council Committee, that if war began, the churches should direct a message to the German people which would assure them that Christians outside Germany distinguished between Nazis and other Germans, and would call on them to do what they could to prevent a Nazi victory. Barth repeated his view openly in a *Letter to the French Protestants* (5 December 1939, also published in English in March 1940), in which he said that 'it would be regrettable if the Christian Churches, which in previous wars have so often and so thoughtlessly spoken the language of nationalism and of militarism, should just in this war equally thoughtlessly decide to adopt the silence of neutralism and pacifism' (p. 34). He added, in a direct challenge to the World Council of Churches: 'Why have the representatives and organs of the ecumenical movement preserved so diplomatic a silence in all these years, and even during the fatal developments of this summer and autumn [1940], as if there were no prophetic ministry of Jesus Christ and as if the Church had no duty of watchfulness?' (p. 35). Barth went on to attack 'voices of an eschatological defeatism which . . . busies itself almost cynically with asserting that

Hitler's present adversaries for their part are no saints either' (p. 35). In a second letter, written to the defeated French in October 1940, Barth said that the Christians in France could not conclude either a peace or an armistice with Hitler: 'in the [Protestant] Church in France . . . even the military armistice which the Vichy Government made with Hitler can only have a provisional character' (p. 51). French Protestants should not accept French Catholic opinions about the war. Barth was calling on the churches to recognise that the war involved more than disputes about territory and material power: it also meant a direct attempt to replace them theologically with the Nazi *Weltanschauung* and so destroy them altogether.

In April 1939, Visser't Hooft had reported Barth's original private approach to Temple. Visser't Hooft himself thought that the churches outside Germany could say that they thought that there was no choice left for most Christians other than resistance to Hitler, but that they could not (as Barth wanted) tell Christians in Germany that they ought to oppose the Nazi regime. Temple replied (21 April 1939) that he was doubtful about saying even this much: 'It is so supremely difficult to avoid making that sort of appeal appear other than hypocritical in the eyes of those to whom it is addressed' (Visser't Hooft, 1973, p. 109). It was true that Barth did not seem to appreciate the contrast between his own comparatively secure exile in Switzerland and the situation of German Christians facing the violence of the Nazis.

Another source of Temple's reservations can be found in the activities of Eivind Berggrav, the Norwegian Primate and Lutheran Bishop of Oslo, who was also a member of the Provisional Council from 1938 to 1948. Berggrav complained to Bell (25 May 1939) that in Barth's approach peace seemed to be identified with Britain and France: 'but what does Christianity tell us about our enemies? Shall we encircle them and unite against them? They feel it as if we are condemning them without recognising our own sins, and without recognising the righteousness and justice in their claims . . .' (Jackson, 1980, p. 261). This was a widespread attitude in which three factors predominated: the belief that the various national churches had gone along too easily with the war of 1914–18; the political judgement, common also in Roman Catholic circles, that Communism, and therefore Russia, was the primary enemy, not Nazism; and genuine anxiety that one was not being sufficiently penitent over past political errors, especially the alleged unfairness towards the Germans of the Versailles treaty. Temple's own reactions to Nazism were confused throughout the 1930s by his failure to recognise that Hitler had drastically changed the context in which the Versailles treaty could be discussed. Barth understood how irrelevantly enervating and close to apathy this kind of guilt-feeling could become. Even Barth's own position was more pietist than political: Nazism must be opposed whatever the consequences, because it was trying to suppress Evangelical Christianity. His political grasp of the situation was much less vivid.

It is significant that one of the more vigorous World Council reactions in 1939–40 was its reply to direct criticism from Germany, where eleven leaders of the Nazi-dominated German Evangelical Church published a declaration (6 April 1939) which stated that Christianity was the religious opposite of Judaism and that supranational 'churchism' in the style of World Protestantism or the Vatican was a political degeneration of Christianity. Stung by this, the Provisional Committee hastened to agree on a reply, and Visser't Hooft had to harmonise drafts from Barth and Temple. Visser't Hooft wrote in his Memoirs that Temple said 'that he had some difficulty in swallowing the phrasing of the combined text, but that he was ready to associate himself with expressions that he would never dream of using on his own account because, unless we were all prepared to do this, there was no hope of full cooperation between British and Continental Churches' (1973, p. 95).

No doubt cooperation was simpler at this theological level, where few practical consequences might be expected to follow. The statement, which was signed by Temple, Boegner, Paton and Visser't Hooft, was printed in The Times on 10 May 1939. Anxious to repudiate the central racialism of the German doctrine, as well as to defend the existence of the embryonic World Council of Churches, Temple had assented to the view that 'the national organization of the Christian Church is not an essential element of its life; it has its blessings, but it has also its dangers'. He was presumably easier with the assertion that the Lordship of Christ was over all areas of life, including politics and ideology, a theological affirmation which hardly meant the same thing to him as it did to Barth.

On Judaism, however, the statement had a dubious ring about it. In order to deny that Judaism and Christianity were opposites the Provisional Committee claimed that 'the gospel of Jesus Christ is the fulfilment of the Jewish hope. The Christian Church owes it, therefore, to the Jewish people to proclaim to it the fulfilment of the promises which have been made to it. And it rejoices in maintaining fellowship with those of the Jewish race who have accepted that gospel.' The traditional terms of this statement disguised from its authors, one suspects, its complacent tone of religious superiority: Christianity might not be the 'unbridgeable opposite to Judaism' which the Germans called it, but its 'gospel of Jesus Christ' made Judaism superfluous. A statement which was agreed quickly because it was supposed to deal with a straightforward theological issue had a political overtone which helps one to understand why life was becoming so dangerous for European Jews in the 1930s. Christianity has never come to terms with the religious survival of Judaism, and even at this most terrible of all the crises in Judaism's history the World Council could not denounce German anti-Semitism without maintaining that fundamentally the Jews survived in order to be converted. Either on Christian or Nazi principles, Jews as Jews ought to disappear.

It is not surprising that when Visser't Hooft visited Britain, France and Holland in October 1939, by which time the so-called Phony War was in full swing, he found himself wondering whether the World Council Provisional Committee had overstressed the idea that the church should not take political or ideological sides. In effect, the drive towards modernisation had stalled at the personal level, the level at which men like Temple and Oldham had assumed that it was easiest to obtain rational agreement.

Another reason for the Provisional Committee's silence during the Second World War can be found in the ironical fact that although the war began with the brief but savage destruction of Poland, there followed some months of inaction – September 1939–April 1940 – in which people waited nervously for a repetition of the carnage of the Great War accompanied by the mass aerial bombardment of cities. This interval was filled with talk about possible peace negotiations: Hitler put out feelers briefly in October; in the same month Pope Pius XII issued the encyclical *Summi Pontificatus*, an appeal for peace on the basis of natural law. In early November Queen Wilhelmina of Holland and King Leopold of Belgium made a joint offer to the King of England to mediate; later in November another go-between, the Swedish businessman Berger Dahlerus made contact on Goering's behalf through the British Embassy in Stockholm. It was also in late November that Josef Müller, who was in touch with the German opposition to Hitler, first contacted the Pope (and so the British government), through Monsignor Kaas, the former, discredited leader of the disbanded German Catholic Centre Party, who was living in exile in Rome. Then at the end of November the sudden Russian attack on Finland excited those for whom Communism was the enemy that counted. Two things seem certain about this period: first, that many people in Britain doubted whether more than economic pressure was needed to defeat Germany; and second, that if Hitler had been removed from power by some internal German movement, Chamberlain and Halifax would have been prepared to negotiate.

This background of intense activity makes it less surprising that the idea of organising a peace intervention should have appealed to Protestant as well as Catholic ecclesiastics. Once again, however, deep divisions inside the World Council Provisional Committee prevented any unified action. As far as Temple was concerned, he had steadily assumed throughout his career that the church, as an institution somehow supplied with divine truth, had socio-political responsibilities which had to be exercised with or without the agreement of the state. Desperately anxious, like so many of his contemporaries, to learn what seemed at the time to be the lessons of the First World War, and still overexcited by the supposed guilt of the Versailles treaty, he began, soon after the Second World War was declared, to try to lay down principles for a better treaty to end the new conflict. In late 1939, when the British and French were taking the defeat of Hitler for granted, it seemed important to assert that victory must not be followed by another allegedly punitive peace, and that during the war itself the churches should not be sucked into national war propaganda systems. Temple, William Paton, J. H. Oldham and others involved in the World Council movement frequently discussed 'peace aims'.

Early in December 1939 some of these pressures came to a

head. On 4 December there appeared in the *Daily Telegraph* a long letter from Temple which appealed to the precedent of Lord Lansdowne's letter (29 November 1917), in which he had asked for a clear definition of the conditions on which the Allies would be prepared to enter into negotiations with the central powers. His hope had been that knowledge of such conditions would encourage the moderate party known to exist in Germany, so that their pressure on the German government might shorten the war. At the time Lansdowne was bitterly attacked as virtually a traitor, but Temple recalled that *Challenge* had said: 'What was there amazing about it, except that it breathed the air of political sanity and Christian hopefulness'? Now he wrote with the same purpose, 'to give confidence to that Germany which Hitler has silenced and wronged'.

There had to be clarity about war aims, he said, because 'all Germany – not only the Nazi regime – considers that the pledges given to the German people by President Wilson before the Armistice of 1918 were violated in important respects by the peace of 1919'. Surely it would be possible for the Allies to agree to an armistice if (a) the Germans would agree to the restoration of genuinely free Polish, Czech and Slovakian states which would take part in the peace conference on an equal footing, and if (b) it were agreed that frontier questions not settled by negotiation 'should be referred for decision to an impartial arbitral body, e.g. one drawn from states which neither gained nor lost from the Peace Treaties of 1919'. There could then be a world conference to establish the foundations of a better international order.

Temple went on to stress the importance of this concept of 'third-party judgement'. The idea of arbitration as a way of settling international disputes was firmly embedded in the Liberal tradition. Temple admitted that its acceptance meant a surrender of complete national sovereignty, but said that this was an essential condition of lasting peace which would open the way to the ultimate goal of a Federal Union. 'It may never be said of any policy that it is the Christian solution in the sense that loyalty to the Christian Faith requires it, but it can be said of Federal Union that it is a Christian solution, because it rests on the recognition that we are fellow members one of another in the family of God.' The attraction of this kind of argument for Temple himself is obvious, but he was aware that such proposals had no chance of being accepted by the Nazi government. Nevertheless, if they were made known, he thought that they would encourage many Germans in their opposition to Hitler. Thus partnership in colonial responsibilities would be open to a Germany which could be relied on never to treat an alien race as the Nazis had treated the Jews.

A letter to his wife suggests that Temple was prompted to write to the *Daily Telegraph* by other supporters of Federal Union, but he had been interested in such schemes for some years, because they fitted into his belief that the future of the world lay in some combination of an ideal British Commonwealth with a world church on the Anglican model. He was to tire of them rapidly, because, as he told the radio philosopher C. E. M. Joad in 1942, 'all of a sudden the idea caught fire and a large number of people seemed to think that Federal Union could be wisely included in a Peace Treaty as the League of Nations Covenant was, and this seems to me a complete delusion' (F. S. Temple, 1963, p. 11).

At the time when he was writing the 'Lansdowne' letter Temple was also involved, through William Paton, with the Bishop of Oslo, Berggrav, who was determined to launch his own 'peace offensive' by combining his ecumenical contacts with others which he had in the German Foreign Office. Paton and Temple invited Berggrav to visit London at the beginning of December, when he saw the Archbishop of Canterbury, who obtained him an interview with the Foreign Secretary, Lord Halifax. Halifax again made clear that the government thought that Hitler's untrustworthiness made negotiations impossible. Undeterred, Berggrav suggested to Temple that at the close of a meeting of the World Council Provisional Committee which had been arranged for the beginning of January there should be a discussion 'chiefly concerned with the concept of peace put forward by the Scandinavians' (Boegner, 1970, p. 138).

The Provisional Committee met on 6–8 January 1940 at De Zilven, near Apeldoorn in Holland, which was still a neutral country. The English representatives were Temple, Bell, Paton and Henry Carter, a prominent Methodist pacifist, whose interest in social questions had brought him into contact with Temple ever since the early 1920s (he had been one of the group which met Baldwin in 1926). There is an extraordinary sentence in Visser't Hooft's Memoirs in which he writes that 'the question was: Should the Churches demand that peace negotiations should take place immediately, and if so, under what conditions?' (1973, p. 118). By now these ecumenical leaders had met in so many conferences and had passed so many resolutions that they easily exaggerated their own importance and the weight of the Protestant and Catholic Churches in European politics. In these strained months, when the British and French governments hoped that time was on their side, Temple's own behaviour sometimes suggests that he had not learned the lesson of his unsuccessful intervention in the Miners' Strike of 1926; it was not difficult to assert a 'Christian' attitude to the conflicts of the day, or to offer oneself as a mediator, but very hard to have oneself taken seriously except as a possible source of useful propaganda. His attitude at this time also testified to the numbing grip which the First World War and its peace treaty still had on the conscience and imagination of the British governing elites.

The course of events at Zilven is not disputed. Berggrav, as a member of a still neutral country, wanted to take to Berlin a conciliatory statement from the World Council of Churches about the conditions under which peace negotiations might be possible. The French Protestant Boegner, supported by Visser't Hooft, for whom the absent Karl Barth's views certainly counted, refused to agree to any negotiation with Hitler: both men thought that the war was a spiritual conflict against a Nazi state which was seeking to impose an anti-Christian ideology. They considered that this threat outweighed any similar danger from Soviet Russia, which was the danger which counted most for Berggrav and for his friends in the Oxford Group, and which was vividly reflected in the plea of a Finnish priest who was present, who said that 'if Finland was to be saved, Germany, France and Britain should come to terms in order to save the christian faith from Bolshevism' (Boegner, 1970, p. 141).

Of the British contingent, Bell, always the soul of political indiscretion, and Carter, one of the pacifists of the 1930s who did not change position once war was declared, were deeply influenced by a simple anxiety to stop the conflict from developing into an all-out war and seem to have had some sympathy with Berggrav. Temple and Paton (with Visser't Hooft's support) were chiefly concerned that 'the church', and particularly the World Council Committee if no larger consensus could be created, should assert that 'Christian civilisation, or a civilisation on the way to becoming Christian', had to be defended against the attacks of Nazism; Christianity was the spiritual core of Western culture, and it was this divinely appointed centrality which entitled the Council to offer public judgements on the issues of war and peace. There was, however, a tension in Temple's mind between his willingness to commit himself and his national church to full support of the nation-in-arms, and his vision of membership in the ecumenical church as being above national differences: the World Council (he thought) should be able to bring Christian opinion together across national boundaries, and even in wartime should try to maintain sympathy between British and German Christians.

Temple had already stumbled into barren arguments when he published the 'Lansdowne' letter. Nevertheless, when Boegner, by refusing to sign any document about negotiations, made an agreed World Council statement impossible, Temple, Bell, Paton and Henry Carter signed a statement of their own which broadly followed the 'Lansdowne' lines in matters of detail. The signatories said that they believed that

it would be right to enter into negotiations if the following points were secured: (a) that the Czech, the Slovak and the Polish peoples be recognised as independent and sovereign – and that practical guarantees for this be forthcoming . . . and (b) that the definitive peace be negotiated in a congress including at least the European nations, the Czechs, the Slovaks and Poles being full partners in the Congress. (Visser't Hooft, 1973, p. 118)

Temple probably thought of himself as doing no more than he had done earlier, that is, offering encouragement to Hitler's German opponents. This new statement was not intended for publication but was apparently taken to the German Foreign Office later in January by Berggrav, who at this point still had neutral status. Nothing whatever came of it.

There was more than a touch of highminded innocence, even of irresponsibility, about this episode, in which pacifism, fear of Communism, Berggrav's interest in the Oxford Group, memories of the Great War, doubts about the Versailles treaty and a mistaken sense of the need for religious leaders to be seen and heard on public affairs were mixed together. The little group of overexcited clergymen at De Zilven were convinced that their overwhelming duty was to prevent the intensification of war if possible. Temple was not the dominant figure: his famous ability to reconcile differences of opinion in international theological conferences was useless in the context of war. Boegner's political firmness was not simply a matter of a theological distinction which could be surmounted by rephrasing a draft statement. Versions of what had happened were reported from Scandinavia, where the impression was given that Temple, Bell and Paton were in favour of peace at any price, and Temple had to publish his own defensive account in February 1940. It was understandable that Iremonger, writing soon after Temple's death, said little about the affair, which may have added to Churchill's later dislike, as Prime Minister, of Temple's appointment as Archbishop of Canterbury.

The participants were not much chastened by their experience, but continued to discuss the subject of war aims in a Christian context. The high point of the process, as far as Temple was concerned, was a letter published on 21 December 1940 in The Times (all concerned had great faith in the value of letters to The Times) which was signed by the Anglican Archbishops, Lang and Temple, by Cardinal Hinsley, and by the Moderator of the Free Church Federal Council, George Armstrong.

The letter's opening paragraph illustrated the extraordinary confidence with which Christian leaders like Temple could survey the modern world. It said that the present evils of the world were due to the failure of nations and peoples to carry out the laws of God. 'No permanent peace is possible in Europe unless the principles of the Christian religion are made the foundation of national polity and of all social life.' The signatories took up five 'peace points' which had been put forward by Pius XII in a Christmas Eve message in 1939, and which the Pope returned to and elaborated in specifically Catholic terms throughout the war without having any obvious effect on the combatants. The Pope suggested that a lasting peace would require guarantees for the integrity of all states, progressive disarmament, an international juridical institution which would be able to enforce a peace treaty once it had been agreed and which would protect minorities, and the development of universal Christian love.

The British ecclesiastics added to the Pope's 'conditions' five much more general points, which were linked to the Ecumenical Movement by their source in the discussions of the Oxford Life and Work Conference held in 1937. The establishment of a lasting peace, it was suggested, required that extreme inequality in wealth and possessions should be abolished; that every child, regardless of race or class, should have equal opportunities of education; that the family as a social unit must be safeguarded; that the sense of a divine vocation must be restored to man's daily work; and that the resources of the earth should be used as God's gifts to the whole human race and with proper consideration for present and future generations. Such an occupation of the high ground could hardly be faulted unless one rejected every kind of economic *dirigisme*, and it contained a substantial part of the Copec policy, which Temple was to relaunch at Malvern in 1941. Although Cardinal Hinsley signed this letter, the spectacle of the English churches speaking with one voice was not to be repeated during the war, and later attempts which Temple made to involve the Vatican in a joint peace-declaration were unsuccessful.

At the start of his chapter on 'The Oecumenical Movement' Temple's official biographer, F. A. Iremonger, placed two quotations from Temple's writings. At his enthronement as

Archbishop of Canterbury in Canterbury Cathedral in April 1942 Temple said of the Ecumenical Movement that 'almost incidentally, the great world-fellowship has arisen; it is the great new fact of our era'; and a year later he wrote with equal confidence:

Our period of history is marked by two contrasted tendencies – one in the secular, one in the Christian realm. The secular world has lost all experience of unity and can do no more than play with the aspiration towards it. The Christian world is moving steadily and rapidly towards deeper unity, and has an actual experience of Christian fellowship across all secular divisions which is full of hope for the future of Christendom and through it for mankind. (Prologue to Is Christ Divided?, 1943)

This was the rhetoric of a man who had arrived and who was confidently explaining what he saw as the world. In fact, the Christian churches, Roman Catholicism included, had not deflected the movement towards catastrophe in 1939–40; the World Council itself, as we have seen, produced no common statement about the Second World War while hostilities lasted; and fifty years later talk about 'the future of Christendom' would sound very strange indeed. The Christian world has not moved steadily and rapidly towards deeper unity. The great new fact in the history of religion, if there is one, would seem to be the accentuated pluralism in the West brought about by the development of non-Christian religious movements. Temple's outlook was conditioned, more than he suspected, by non-religious beliefs in the solidity of British power and the permanence of some kind of British Empire, itself related to the continuing dominance of Western socio-political ideas. Perhaps, in any case, Temple exaggerated the value of Protestantism's being able to speak through a central voice, a constitutional papacy. The history of the papacy is not a simple recommendation of such institutions.

Nevertheless, Temple's vision of a modernised and united Protestantism which would be warmly open to further ecumenical progress made political sense in a 'Christendom' deeply divided by the social and ethical conservatism of official Roman Catholicism; it also made secular political sense, as every aspect of human life was subjected to international organisation. On the ecumenical stage, Temple had conceived this initial modernisation of the churches in terms reminiscent of the organisation of the SCM or of the world missionary societies. There would be a representative central committee which would support a permanent General Secretary with a headquarters staff located, in this instance, in Geneva: Life and Work and Faith and Order would continue to develop as part of this Genevan base. In the long run, which was not specifically Temple's business, the member churches might become national provinces of a global 'church'. Such an institution had obvious attractions for would-be ecclesiastics and opinion-formers.

# Chapter 3

# The church in politics

## COPEC

The setting-up of the Church Assembly, which held its first meeting in 1920, did not inaugurate a rapid internal modernisation of the Church of England. As the *Spectator* had expected, a body of ecclesiastically minded lay representatives with limited financial powers was broadly satisfied with the leadership offered by episcopal government in the 1920s. Temple gradually realised that increased Anglican liberty had not intensified Anglican life, and already in 1919 he had taken the first steps which led to the Conference on Christian Politics, Economics and Citizenship (Copec), which was held at Birmingham from 5 to 12 April 1924. Through this Conference, which has been widely regarded as a major achievement on Temple's part, he hoped to guide not only the Church of England but all the British churches towards common political action over a field which stretched from international relations to the organisation of industry. He was not trying to subordinate the English churches to any particular party, but to argue that the religious and political aspects of the life of the community should not be separated, that the nation should once again move towards the goal of becoming a Christian commonwealth.

In the brief period of postwar excitement even Roman

Catholics took part in the production of the reports on which the Copec meetings were based. They registered dissent whenever doubt was cast on official Catholic views, and they dropped out shortly before the Conference met, perhaps because the fruitless Malines Conversations between Anglican and Roman Catholic theologians, which had started in 1921 and were the first such meetings since the sixteenth century, were dividing the English Catholic Church. The Catholic withdrawal underlined the old-fashioned side of Temple's vision of a church establishment justified by a political unification of the British churches under Anglican leadership, but he was ahead of his contemporaries in seeing that Christian unity was one, if not necessarily the best, response to the social pluralism of the future.

In practice, a Copec Council of 350 members with Temple as chairman was set up in 1920, and twelve commissions produced book-length reports which were more important than the Conference itself. These dealt with The Nature of God and his Purpose for the World, Education, The Home, The Relation of the Sexes, Leisure, The Treatment of Crime, International Relations, Christianity and War, Industry and Property, Politics and Citizenship, The Social Function of the Church (which largely duplicated some of the previous discussion) and Historical Illustrations of the Social Effects of Christianity. These books summed up one side of the social thinking which had gone on in the English churches since the beginning of the nineteenth century, and nothing quite like them has appeared since. The commissions put forward resolutions which the actual Conference, consisting of about 1,400 delegates, slightly modified.

The Birmingham Conference was held towards the close of a chaotic period in national politics which stretched from 1918 to the General Strike of 1926. In these years the wartime coalition government collapsed, Lloyd George was castrated politically, and the Liberal Party was effectively replaced as the official Opposition by the Labour Party, which formed a minority administration early in 1924 and was still in office while the Conference was taking place. Finally, a rejigged Conservative Party emerged, in which opposition to socialism was combined with Baldwin's gentrified 'English' nationalism, an elegy from the churchyard of rural England. Traditional Conservatives understood the limits of progress in the hands of the Liberals, guessed that the Labour Party was not revolutionary, but feared the trade unions as a new extra-parliamentary centre of power. The drive to restrict that power was to continue down to Margaret Thatcher's anti-union legislation of the 1980s. The political situation did not favour the kind of vague but radical social transformation which the Copec delegates had in mind.

How far social change might go was unclear after the war of 1914–18, and especially after the Russian Revolution of 1917, but there was a stage at which Temple might have been forgiven for thinking that in the Church of England itself he was pushing at an open door. The lacklustre, internally divided National Mission of 1916 had led the Archbishops to set up fresh committees on the church's relation to the outside world, the most famous of which reported in 1918 in a radical volume called *Christianity and Industrial Problems*. As ecclesiastical committees went, this one was radical: the Chairman was the Bishop of Winchester, E. S. Talbot, together with the Bishop of Oxford, Charles Gore, the Bishop of Peterborough, F. T. Woods, and the Bishop of Lichfield, J. A. Kempthorne; the laymen included the Labour politician George Lansbury, as well as two of Temple's closest associates, Albert Mansbridge and R. H. Tawney. Their report said that the fundamental evil of modern industrialism was that it encouraged competition for private gain instead of cooperation for public service, a judgement heard in Anglican intellectual circles from about 1850. This perversion of motive fostered an organisation of industry which treated workers as hands instead of as persons. The poverty which the system produced could not simply be attributed to the personal defects of individuals, still less to natural scarcity. There was, moreover, an attitude of mutual antagonism and suspicion between the different sides of industry. The report said categorically that the concept of industry as a selfish competitive struggle was unchristian. Industry should be regarded primarily as a social service, based on the effort of every individual to fulfil his duty to his neighbour and to the community. The report recommended the principle of the living wage, unemployment insurance and the setting-up of an industrial parliament. (This last was a possibility often discussed between the two World Wars, but a non-starter because the political class that operated through Parliament was determined not to give up any of its power.) There was no question of such far from politically neutral proposals becoming official Anglican 'policy', but the Fifth Report was accepted as one of the bases on which the Birmingham Conference worked.

The increasing Anglican popularity of criticism of the economic system was not entirely a matter of fashions in 'progressive' thinking. By 1914, what worried many Anglicans (and also, significantly, some right-wing secular politicians) was not so much economic competition as the increasing political competition of the classes which had been created by it. This anxiety was one of the features of the 1917 Selborne Report on church and state. Selborne drew a distinction between the 'workers' and 'the administrative classes'. It said that 'it is futile to close one's eyes to the fact that the greater solidarity of the workers is making it possible for them to force their claims upon any government, and it is probably not an exaggeration to say that never in the world's history has it been more necessary than at present to enlist the active sympathies of the great mass of the people on the side of religion and order, if the recognised standards of civilisation are to be maintained'. On the other side, the report said that the administrative classes were 'largely ignorant of the modern spirit and the aspirations of the workers, and they underrate the ethical driving force of the revolutionary ideas, and are apt to regard labour aspirations with hostility and suspicion rather than with sympathy and hope. This separation of the classes is a national calamity' (Selborne, 1917, pp. 256–7).

More than one political or religious group could agree to such sentiments: the appeal to 'religion and order' and to 'the recognised standards of civilisation', the dread of separation between the classes as though in the past they had somehow been united in a peaceful deference-society – these were familiar themes in the centre and on the right. Such a passage limits the scope of E. R. Norman's argument that many twentieth-century Anglican leaders substituted unsound secular notions of progress for the healthy realism of orthodox theology. Fear of social disorder, of trade union power, of changing moral standards, of the end of 'civilisation' could also prompt an Anglican search for ways of conciliating working-class hostility, and such motives explain much in Copec. The same anxieties also help to explain the episcopal popularity of the Industrial Christian Fellowship, which was to be closely associated with Temple. It was started in 1919 with J. A. Kempthorne as its chairman. The ICF's chief missioner was a former Army chaplain, Studdert Kennedy, a popular revivalist whose social views were similar to E. R. Norman's own, and whose aim was to change the working classes politically by religious conversion, a slow way of preventing revolution. Kennedy did not think of himself as propping up the established order: he thought of himself as rising above it.

Not all Anglicans were moved to conciliate, however. When Kempthorne supported striking railwaymen in a letter to The Times in 1919, Hensley Henson, who feared unionism, commented bitterly in his journal that 'the clerical toadies of this age do not flatter princes but mobs. And the reason is the same. They worship the possessors of power' (Henson, 1942, p. 316, cf. Norman, 1976, p. 256). In March 1923 Davidson even considered resignation, on the ground that he was out of sympathy with the fashion for social theology. In the end he remained Archbishop until the failure of his Prayer Book reform policy left him no option but to retire. In the 1920s Temple's own attitude was to the left of the religious centre-right, which itself varied all the way from the humane conservatism of an Anglican politician like Lord Robert Cecil to the Maurassian anti-Semitism of Hilaire Belloc, whose repulsive polemic, The Jews, was published in 1922. Temple tried to spread his own ideas more widely through The Pilgrim, a quarterly which he edited from 1920 to 1927. In January 1921, he wrote, much in the spirit which animated Lloyd George's opponents in the Conservative Party, that 'opportunism is triumphant. Political life is directed according to no intelligible principles and towards no distinguishable goal'. More importantly, in January 1923 he rejected Conservatism of the type which argued that the state could check evil but could do little positive good; that one could, for example, prevent the employment of children in mines and factories but that one could not develop public control as a successful alternative to private enterprise. Temple also rejected theological utopianism, the setting out of an ideal Christian state, on the ground that the New Testament gave no detailed account of this which would be of any use in modern terms.

Despite this conclusion, Temple thought that it was possible to find permanently valid principles of social conduct in the New Testament. 'The Gospel being a proclamation of the true nature of God and Man and of the true relationship between them, necessarily consists of principles from which some others may with perfect security be deduced.' Among these principles were, as we would expect to learn from Temple, freedom and respect for personality, fellowship, the duty of service and the power of sacrifice. Such ideas were not in themselves the stuff of a political programme, 'but it is at least conceivable', he said – and one notes that he was no longer saying that one could arrive at one's conclusions 'with perfect security' – 'that Christianity may have much to say in general terms about the right of wage earners to be consulted on all decisions of management affecting their own lives, about the quantity of leisure to be rightly claimed by a man engaged in purely mechanical work'. Temple's claim that he was not talking about programmes was all very well, but in practice the assertion that workers had a right to share in making management decisions involved a radical departure from British industrial tradition and one still resisted by British businesspeople in the 1980s, when 'the right to manage' was a battlecry.

If Temple sometimes seems very uncritical in his appeals to the authority of the New Testament, one has to remember that the leading Anglican theologians of the 1920s had matured in an atmosphere of mutual confirmation, accepting that the New Testament was a unique divine revelation, even if what was revealed was simultaneously hidden in a historical text which required expert manipulation. He thought that the Copec movement itself should proceed from primary gospel principles to secondary principles which would offer effective guidance over the whole of contemporary life. That these secondary principles, sometimes called middle axioms, were not universally accepted as 'Christian' was made evident when the Roman Catholics who had worked on the various reports withdrew from Copec. In the case of the report on *Industry and Property*, for example, the Roman Catholic committee member, Ada Streeter, dissented from the final version, claiming that 'the stress laid on "equality" is liable to grave misinterpretation incompatible with Catholic principle; that the blame for our present difficulties does not lie wholly with Employers, Proprietors and Industrialists; that some mention should have been made of the dangers arising from extremist and revolutionary propaganda' (Copec, 1924, p. 199). At the Copec assembly itself in 1924, the guidance derived indirectly from the New Testament became quite detailed: the delegates accepted resolutions which called for workers to have a share in the direction of industry, and for a living wage which was more than a bare minimum.

One suspects that many of those present did not think of these resolutions as having the practical implications which Temple attached to them and which critics like Henson exploited. In *Quo Tendimus* (1924), a Primary Charge to his diocesan clergy in which he bitterly denounced Copec, Henson said that it was fundamental in Christ's religion that the redemption of the world must be effected through the redemption of individuals. Many of the Copec delegates would probably have agreed with Henson: personal conversion was the emotional basis of their Christianity; they supported the Copec resolutions as a moral gesture, not as a political act; and what interested them most at the practical level was legislation to restrict drinking, gambling, contraception and prostitution, the familiar targets of the late Victorian 'Social Gospel'. In these areas the views of the Copec majority were not 'progressive' at all. Temple, on the other hand, always thought of 'the redemption of the world' as meaning the conversion of individuals within the framework of a society which was also being redeemed, and he regarded the Copec reports as the foundation documents of a Christian pressure-group.

The success of the Copec Conference from Temple's point of view has been exaggerated: it did not lay the basis for a powerful movement in the 1920s and 1930s. The causes of his relative failure can already be seen at work before the Conference opened. The Davidson Correspondence at Lambeth shows that from 1921 onwards Temple and his Copec assistants, Lucy Gardner, who was a Quaker, and Charles Raven, another of the young Anglican priests who had been permanently scarred by their wartime experience, kept up a steady pressure on the Archbishop to persuade him to give Copec official standing, and that Davidson sinuously but steadily refused. Once again, as in the Life and Liberty years, Temple seemed to Davidson to be trying to take control of Anglican policy, to create a momentum which would commit the Church of England to radical social attitudes. Temple understood the Archbishop's horror of clearly defined social policies, but he explained (15 June 1921) that what he hoped for from the Copec discussions was 'the assertion of some principles by a really representative body, [principles] which would be more explicit than the great platitudes and less particular than a political programme'. What mattered was the assembling of a 'really representative body', and it was here that Temple could not persuade the Archbishop to help him. Davidson declined to support Temple's suggestion that the two Anglican Convocations should send delegations; he refused to speak at a preparatory Albert Hall meeting laid on in 1923; he refused (in October 1923) to attend the Conference itself, let alone address it. Only just before the Birmingham meetings began in April 1924 did he give Temple a tepid message of greeting.

Davidson was not simply defending his own authority. He knew that there was no serious question of Temple attempting to found a Christian-democratic political party, though he may have wondered whether his aim was not to make the Church of England as devoted to the Labour Party as the Nonconformists had been to the pre-1914 Liberal Party. Davidson did not share Temple's vision of the English churches, or the Anglican church, or at worst a part of the Anglican church, entering the political field as an independent pressure-group with a policy drawn as much from New Liberal as from New Testament or socialist sources – and this was what Temple wanted, not just an official Board of Social Responsibility which might formulate 'principles' and publish reports on which no one acted. From the Archbishop's point of view, Temple was contradicting the political wisdom of many of his Anglican elders, who had concluded from their pre-1914 experience that the wisest plan for the Church of England was to avoid political exposure, accepting that Parliament had shown its weariness with the English state church by disestablishing the church in Wales. From this point of view the purpose of the Enabling Act had been to facilitate a retreat into spiritual, not political, independence. Davidson did not put unemployment at the top of his agenda for the 1920s; instead, he hoped to improve the Anglican public image by settling the conflict between Anglo-Catholic and Evangelical for control of the services in the parish church.

Temple's opening address to the Birmingham Conference (he sent an advance copy to Davidson) could not have conciliated the Archbishop. Temple said that the Conference represented 'a great movement within the Church which is, I am convinced, a movement of the Holy Ghost'. For centuries, most Christians had lost the vision of the Kingdom of God as claiming the allegiance of all nations and authority over all departments of life, but since the mid nineteenth century that claim had been vigorously reasserted, and now one was witnessing the convergence of a 'spiritual movement in the Church prompted by loyalty and hope, and a spiritual movement in the world prompted by disillusion and despair'. This inaccurate statement was followed by much about the need for 'repentance', but it was significant emotionally that the first direct reference to contemporary issues was to unemployment: 'we bear on our hearts the burden of unemployment, and in our consciences the challenge which tells us that where such things happen God's Kingdom is not yet come on earth as it is in Heaven'. To this he added anxiety about peace, and about those 'who have fallen into crime or are victims of lust'. The address was wrapped in Edwardian religious rhetoric for an audience still balanced between pre- and postwar attitudes.

Temple's opening speech asserted that he had the support of the Holy Ghost; his concluding statement (12 April 1924) outlined the programme. The Conference called 'on all Christian people to do all in their power to find and apply the remedy for recurrent unemployment, to press vigorously for the launching of efficient housing schemes, whether centrally or locally, and to secure an immediate extension of educational facilities, especially for the unemployed adolescents, whose case is perhaps the most deplorable of all the deplorable features of our social life today . . . we urge the immediate raising of the school leaving age to sixteen, and the diminution as rapidly as possible of the maximum size of classes'. The moral ambiguity of many delegates' attitudes to the British Empire and British industry was visible in a resolution urging Christians to do their utmost to prevent the introduction of 'our own industrialism' into Asia or Africa (Temple Papers, vol. 14).

One reason why, apart from its level of generality, this programme was not translated into a movement was that the

Conference itself was not as unanimously progressive as has sometimes been suggested. The Conference declaration, for example, did not suggest a remedy for unemployment. In the vital area of sexual ethics passionate discussion about contraception only produced a call for further investigation, and no agreed line emerged on divorce. The pietist resolutions in The Home were strengthened by a backward-glancing plea for daily family worship, and the only change to the resolutions in Leisure was a demand for a 'diminution of licences' in the section on drink. It is true that the Conference added to The Treatment of Crime support for the abolition of the death penalty, but the final form of the key resolution on Christianity and War left the question of pacifism undecided, saying that 'all war is contrary to the spirit and teaching of Jesus Christ, and that therefore in time of war more than ever the Church of Christ must witness and labour for the Christian way of life against hatred and cruelty'. In its historical context this was a reaction against the religious nationalism of the Great War. There were extremists at Birmingham, like the member of the Hull Christian Social Council who called for censorship of the cinema. This was an indication that the Conference contained many pietists (Free church as well as Anglican) who were more concerned about regulating private behaviour than about creating a fairer economic society.

The inner contradictions of the Conference, and therefore the limits of Temple's success, become clearer if one looks at the two most important reports, Politics and Citizenship (vol. 10) and Industry and Property (vol. 9). Politics and Citizenship was produced by a committee which included Lord Eustace Percy, Maurice Reckitt, J. R. M. Butler, Lady Parmoor (whose husband was one of the Liberals who helped Ramsay MacDonald in 1924), Hugh Martin of the Student Christian Movement, and Ruth Kenyon, who, like Reckitt, was a member of the Anglo-Catholic League of the Kingdom of God.

The fate of *Politics and Citizenship* at the Birmingham meeting showed the limits of Temple's belief that one could translate the biblical text into generally agreed first principles. The first resolution in the printed report made the biblically plausible but politically naive assertion, which Temple had always taken for granted as the basis of his case for establishment, that 'the authority of the State has a divine sanction . . . it can demand obedience in God's name . . . The state is ordained by God for the purpose of binding men together in a justly ordered social life . . . and ought only to be challenged in the name of God.' To his amazement this statement was challenged at Birmingham, and as chairman he had to rule out of order an amendment which pointed out the ambiguous nature of state-power in history. The final version went no further than saying that the state's authority 'ought to be generally accepted by Christians, and ought to be challenged by the Christian conscience only in the name of God'. In its immediate context this conflict echoed the bitter wartime debate about conscription, which the Gladstonian Liberals had resisted but which Temple had justified.

Much of the report had a strongly individualistic flavour: the discussion was about what the individual Christian should do. There was no real suggestion of 'social services' in the post-1950 sense, but 'social service' was thought of in the traditional manner as individual Christian charity. One has to remember that the churches had recently been legislated out of some of their Edwardian social activities, such as the provision of school meals in some parts of London. Significantly, the tone of the report did not allow for the possibility of a humanist source of social service: school meals provided by secular local government would amount to socialism and would have no spiritual value. The broad case which was being made for Christianity turned on the argument that only religion could generate the necessary moral enthusiasm and insight required for social work.

There was an effort to balance the report's overriding individualism by the assertion that 'Social Service means a common effort to secure a better life; it does not mean the assistance of one class by another. Social Service is necessarily concerned with the whole life, and therefore all forms of service are interdependent. The Health, Education, Employment and Recreation of the Community are all the concern of every Christian member of the Community' (Politics and Citizenship, p. 106). These were characteristic Temple-concepts: on the one hand, the ideal of a Christian 'Social Service' which would emerge from the religious community and make unnecessary the professional social worker whom we actually have in the 1990s; on the other, a recognition that in the twentieth century 'social service' might mean not just the individual charity of the better-off towards the less fortunate, but a concerted drive to reduce inequality in the areas of education, employment, recreation and health. There was a hint of criticism here of the Helen Bosanquet and Charity Organisation Society style of 'social work' with its stress on 'character' and on the need to restrict relief to the 'deserving poor', but Mrs Bosanquet's manifesto, The Strength of the People (1902), was referred to in the report as a 'noble work', and neither the Copec Conference nor Temple envisaged schemes for the unconditional relief of poverty or the provision of a health service funded largely by taxation and with equal access for all. The National Health Service, as it developed after 1945, may have been more 'Christian' than schemes of contractual social insurance, but if so, Copec was not responsible. There was only the vaguest adumbration of a 'welfare state', however defined, at this stage.

The result was a report which implied that Christian

citizenship was more a matter of personal choice than collective action. In calling Copec together Temple had said that he did not want a Christian political party, but a Christian presence in all parties. There was little else that one could say in England in the 1920s, when even the much more deliberately political papacy was still resisting the formation of a Catholic Party in Italy, and preserving clerical control of the Centre Party in Germany. Consequently, the section of the report which dealt with 'The Church and Parties' (Politics, pp. 42–7) said that the church could not take sides politically. Only one member of the committee, Ruth Kenyon, at odds with the rest of the Christendom group, recorded dissent, saying that 'the Church should throw its weight on the side of that party [Labour] which challenges the existing social and industrial system' (Politics, p. 107). The weakness of her argument was that the leadership of the churches could not command their members politically: to attempt to identify the rank and file with one political party would simply have split them, as had happened in the case of Methodism and the Liberal Party. Temple, who never lost his hope that the rank and file could be persuaded to see that 'the church's faith' compelled it to work collectively for greater social equality, tried to solve the problem by creating a political programme for the use of a Christian pressure-group. One effect of the First World War, however, had been to encourage political groups which sought to extend the power of the state, and this in turn drove individualistic religious Liberals towards the Conservatives and reduced Temple's chances of building a coalition of Christians on the centre and left.

The report was much happier denouncing the 'Evils of the Press and Public Opinion', and calling on the churches to foster a public opinion 'which will no longer tolerate the undue prominence given to sensational details of the divorce courts and of sordid vice, the incentives to wholesale betting and gambling, the vulgarity of much advertisement, and the exaltation of false values, which at present largely distort much in modern journalism and magazines'.

If *Politics and Citizenship* represented the conservative core of Copec, *Industry and Property* represented the radical margin. What emerged was a rough sketch of an alternative, more equal society. Even here the Conference had doubts: the printed text of the report said that in industry and commerce Christians should aim at 'the substitution of the motive of service for the motive of gain', but at Birmingham the aim was altered to procuring 'the predominance of the motive of service'. Industry, it was said, should become a 'cooperative effort adequately to supply the needs of all . . . this does not involve one particular type of organization universally applied'; all those who worked in industry should have a voice in running it. This may be compared with what Temple himself said in 1942 in *Christianity and Social Order* when, after rejecting the schemes for common ownership which Sir Richard Acland had proposed at Malvern, he said that the task was to get the best out of both individualism and socialism, adding that 'the art of government is . . . to secure that the lower motives actually found among men prompt that conduct which the high motives demand' (Temple, 1942, p. 100). The 1924 report said that the first charge on industry should be a decent living wage for the ordinary worker, not the interests of the shareholders. Finally, 'the evils of unemployment are intolerable to the moral sense. The causes must be sought and removed.' The context of this last resolution was slum property, with its attendant problems of poor health and education.

'Extremes of wealth and poverty', the report continued, 'are likewise intolerable. A Christian order involves a juster distribution.' The moral justification of the rights of property was said to be the degree to which they contributed 'to the development of personality and to the good of the whole community'. If they failed to serve these purposes, the rights of property should be modified or abolished. In effect, 'the duty of service is equally obligatory upon all. No inherited wealth or position can dispense any member of the Christian society from establishing by service his claim to maintenance' (*Industry and Property*, pp. 194–5). In 1942 Temple gave a practical turn to this criticism of inherited industrial wealth by proposing to limit the inheritance of dividends.

E. R. Norman distinguished between these generous but not necessarily Christian ideas – after all, William Morris had said something similar in *News from Nowhere* – and the results of Temple's Malvern Conference in 1941. He argued that the papers given at Malvern were quite unlike the Copec reports of 1924, because the Malvern Conference was theological, whereas Copec had attempted to describe social policies. For Norman the importance of *Christianity and Social Order* (1942), which Temple published after Malvern, lay in its cautiousness and reservations, and the way in which Temple separated his political programme from the Christian principles which he advocated in the main body of the book (Norman, 1976, p. 366). Norman (and also A. M. Suggate) argued that social radicalism had been eclipsed in the Anglicanism of the 1940s by the influence of theologians like Reinhold Niebuhr and the émigré Russian Orthodox theologian Nicholas Berdyaev, whose *Slavery and Freedom* (1939; English translation, 1943) suggested to Norman a 'disillusionment with human nature as represented in liberal thinking, and with all the barrenness of Humanism' (Norman, 1976, p. 364). Berdyaev, however, said that contact with the West had sent him back to the socialism of his youth: 'I do not believe in the aristocracy of a group, in an aristocracy which is founded on social assortment. There is nothing more repellent than contempt for the mass of the people among those who regard themselves as an elite' (Berdyaev, 1943, p. 18). Berdyaev, in fact, was much closer to Temple than he was to the elitist Christian politics which emanated from the discussions of Oldham, T. S. Eliot, Karl Mannheim and others in their private discussion-club, The Moot, a religious equivalent of the cultural elitism of Clive Bell, who declared that 'civilisation' was always the product of a leisured minority supported by a servant/slave majority (see his *Civilisation*, 1928). Tawney had replied to him in *Equality* (1931), and Berdyaev took the same side in 1939: 'You cannot refuse to solve the problem of daily bread for the labouring masses on the ground that when this problem was not solved and while the masses were oppressed culture was very beautiful. Especially is this impossible for christians' (Berdyaev, 1943, p. 18).

The difference between Copec and both the Malvern Conference and the Penguin Special was not in this theoretical area, but rather in the absence in 1941/2 of that vision, which had seemed so vivid in 1924, of a Christian society which would have exhibited an austere cult of service, simplicity and cooperation. This had many roots, among them the Anglican public-school ethos of the late nineteenth century, the private asceticism of Anglo-Catholics and Evangelical pietists and the cool Quaker insistence on rational extremes. Copec was told that 'we feel that there is a strong challenge to all Christians to work out a better standard of life which would not only in theory but in practice make better but less costly living more possible. There are already many modest homes of leaders in art, literature, science, the professions and the churches which go far to prove that the best culture and social intercourse are not nearly so expensive as is generally supposed, but well within the reach of a society that would in comparison with existing conditions be reckoned as poor' (*Industry and Property*, p. 116).

This was a narrow basis from which to attempt to control society.

Where Dr Norman seems to be right about Copec is in his judgement that 'the bishops had managed to miscalculate the public mood. To the extent that their adoption of social radicalism was a hopeful overture to the masses it fell flat; to the extent that it annoyed the laity, who objected to clerical interference, it was a nuisance. But they had no alternative, for there can be no doubt that their social moralism was not calculated, but really did arise from their own heightened sense of social concern' (Norman, 1976, p. 260). Norman's conclusion, that the Copec programme proved unattractive outside and inside the churches, is convincing. There was already a feeling at Copec itself that 'social radicalism' had lost the initiative. In *Politics and Citizenship*, for example, one finds the defiant assertion that 'in spite of . . . the mental lassitude and the social and political disappointment of the last few years, we are convinced that the mind in which Christian people emerged from the war represents still their deepest thought on these questions. That mind is one of deep desire and strong determination to make an end of the types of social arrangement which breed ill-will, unrest and strife. It is a mind of deep faith that in Christianity we have possession of the principles which can show us the better way.' This was partly wishful thinking, partly recognition that 'Christian people' disagreed about how to deal with social conflict.

This did not mean the complete disappearance of the radical side of the Copec tradition. The radicalism of some of the reports was not just the product of abstract agreement between ecclesiastics and intellectuals with the same social background: Temple's driving-force, for example, was the relative failure of free enterprise in some parts of the country after 1918, the sheer quantity of poverty, undereducation, poor housing, ill-health and unemployment which persisted into the 1930s, exacerbated by the Great Crash of 1929. On the whole, however, worsening conditions reinforced the ethical individualism of the Christian churches, and plans to form a movement on the basis of the Copec Conference quietly petered out. A fundamental weakness of all the Copec reports was their confidence that Christianity introduced new spiritual factors into the socio-political equation, that is, not only a new vision of society but also a new community able to release spiritual power in support of these ideas. This was not the case.

Any hopes that the secular political system might be influenced by the Copec approach almost vanished in the wake of Labour's overwhelming defeat in the 1931 election. What became clear in the later 1920s was how little right-wing politicians and industrialists were prepared to concede to organised labour, and what a firm grip they had on much middle-class opinion: their resistance led to the General Strike, middle-class reaction against the strike, and then to the failure of the continuing miners' strike in 1926. There was a serious struggle for dominance, in which the defeat of the trade unions was more important than the existence of minority MacDonald governments, consciously and publicly non-revolutionary, for part of 1924 and at the close of the decade. Temple and many of his associates at Copec were anxious that in this political situation the churches should not simply be seen by organised labour and the unemployed as lined up in spiritual support of material wealth, but by 1931 this had become the politics of the unsuccessful gesture. Given this background the General Strike was the decisive event of the 1920s for 'Christian socialism', because it made clear that the majority of 'churchpeople' wanted social peace more than they wanted social change.

## THE GENERAL STRIKE 1926

The General Strike of 3–12 May 1926 was not, as far as the Trades Union Congress was concerned, a revolutionary attack on the constitution – though it suited some right-wing politicians to say that it was. It was the moment at which the Conservative government faced down an attempt of the trade union movement to alter the postwar balance of economic and social power: as a result, serious structural change was postponed until 1945. The postwar coal industry was in decline; in 1919 a royal commission (the Sankey) had even reported in favour of nationalisation. The mine-owners not only rejected this, but by 1926 were demanding a reduction in wages together with an alteration of the law which would permit a lengthening of the working day. A second royal commission (the Samuel) reported in March 1926, dismissing nationalisation, any further state subsidy, and the idea of a longer day. The owners ignored the report. The miners would not accept both lower wages and longer hours, and so were locked out on 1 May 1926. The Trades Union Congress, which had promised to support the miners and was afraid that a precedent was being set for a more general industrial campaign to reduce wages, began a general strike, but this enabled the government to appeal successfully for middle-class support. The union leaders backed down when they realised that neither the government (which put on an impressive display of military and naval strength) nor the employers had any intention of offering a compromise, and that middle-class (including Anglican) sympathy would not stretch beyond charity to political pressure. The miners, not for the last time exaggerating the impact of their industrial action, were isolated, and finally capitulated in the autumn.

The General Strike did not affect Temple directly, because he was in Europe at the time being treated for gout. He wrote to Davidson offering his services, but the Archbishop replied on 10 May, when the General Strike was almost over, that he did not think there was anything to be gained by Temple's changing his plans. This was true: nothing positive had come of Davidson's own interventions. On 5 May in the House of Lords he called the General Strike unwise and intolerable and said that the government must end it; in a milder statement issued on 7 May over his own name as an 'appeal from the Churches' he in effect asked all parties to return to the negotiating table without preconditions, a suggestion which was politically irrelevant. His request to broadcast this appeal to the nation was refused by Reith, the Director-General of the BBC, who sagaciously concealed the government advice to which he had yielded. With his habitual caution, Davidson stopped short of saying that the strike was an act of rebellion (see especially an article inspired from Lambeth which appeared in the St Martin's Review, 20 June 1926). In the aftermath Davidson received a letter (19 May) from a group of MPs which included Nancy Astor, Noel Buxton, Alfred Salter and Henry Slesser, which told him that he had 'brought to the forefront the Christian bearings of industrial problems, the Christian spirit that should be cherished in their consideration, and the Christian solutions that must be attempted in the great work of reconstruction that now lies before the country' (Davidson Papers, vol. 273). Many Anglicans, however, including Henson and Inge, preferred Cardinal Bourne's declaration in a sermon on 9 May that the General Strike 'was a direct challenge to a lawfully consti-tuted authority . . . a sin against the obedience which we owe to God' (Oldmeadow, 1944, pp. 215–30). It is unlikely that Temple would have been able to alter the impression that most church leaders disliked the apparent increase in the power of organised labour. What Temple did not fully grasp, perhaps because he was out of England at the critical time, was the determination of the employers to impose their conditions on the mining unions, and the reluctance of Baldwin's government to prevent them from doing so.

When Temple returned to England, he became involved in a fresh ecclesiastical démarche designed to lessen the gap between the churches and the miners. Davidson, after his experiences during the General Strike, was unwilling to risk the prestige of his office any further. It is true that at the end of May he said that he would watch for any chance to throw 'such weight as we possess into the arguments in favour of conference and negotiation' (Davidson to Chisholm, 26 May 1926), but the weight was never thrown, and he declined to join an appeal for money for the miners' families. As a result, there emerged a more or less self-appointed 'Standing Conference of the Christian Churches on the Coal Dispute' (it could have done with a humbler title), half Anglican and half Nonconformist, whose chairman was Kempthorne, and most of whose secretarial work was done by P. T. R. Kirk, both of the Industrial Christian Fellowship. Together with Kirk, Temple renewed pressure begun by Kempthorne in May to persuade Davidson that, as a gesture towards the miners, the Ecclesiastical Commissioners should give up what they received on behalf of the Church of England in mining royalties. Davidson thought that this amounted to about £300,000 a year, and he was worried about the situation of incumbents whose benefices were endowed from this income. Temple wrote to Davidson (4 June 1926), proposing to move a resolution at the Church Assembly in July expressing the hope that the Commissioners (over whom the Assembly had no control) would facilitate any steps which government might take to nationalise the royalties.

Once again, Davidson blunted the issue. Replying on 9 June 1926, he told Temple that the Estates Committee of the

Ecclesiastical Commissioners had already told the Prime Minister privately that if it could be shown 'that state ownership of the minerals would conduce to the prosperity of the industry and advance the national interest it would be their duty to refrain from opposition to any scheme of state purchase based upon fair compensation'. They had said that despite their objections to nationalisation in principle, they would not, in such circumstances, resist. This was a formula which gave little away beyond the admission that if the state decided to act, the coal-owners, including the Commissioners, would have to give way. Davidson suggested that Temple's resolution should take the form of 'expressing the Assembly's satisfaction that the Estates Commission had already intimated its readiness to accept such a scheme' (Davidson Papers, vol. 273). Temple (11 June 1926) agreed to a procedure in which the Archbishop would indicate the position of the Ecclesiastical Commissioners, after which he would withdraw his original resolution. Nothing would happen about the Anglican income from mining royalties, nor had anything positive been done to suggest Anglican concern about the striking miners.

Just before the meeting of the Church Assembly Temple was back with an even less successful and much less sophisticated suggestion. He wrote to Davidson (2 July 1926) quoting a Lancashire coal-owner who remembered how in 1893 Lord Rosebery settled a long coal dispute by getting the owners and union leaders together over a champagne lunch. Temple and his friend had discussed who could work such a miracle now: Baldwin might not want to, they had thought of Balfour and Asquith, but best of all would be the Archbishop himself – or he might persuade the Lord Mayor of London. Davidson, in line with his earlier policy, declined in a prompt answer (3 July 1926): 'I am certain I act rightly in keeping myself to general principles of the need for a conciliatory policy and not attempting to intervene myself as to what the negotiations ought to be.'

Temple's proposal was an essay in Anglican romanticism, not politics, but by this time the Church of England was suffering from Davidson's determination to go on being Archbishop in his seventies. In effect he was refusing to take a not inconsiderable group of his bishops seriously. Moreover, it has not always been recognised that the 'Standing Conference' also included a very representative set of Free church leaders, among them M. E. Aubrey, who was the Secretary of the Baptist Union, S. M. Berry, the Secretary of the Congregational Union, W. F. Lofthouse, who was Principal of the Wesleyan Theological College in Birmingham, Henry Carter, the most influential Methodist in the social field, and W. S. Nicholson of the Society of Friends. No doubt in Davidson's eyes these were not great men, and no doubt they were anxious to maintain the waning claim of the Free churches to be in touch with the working classes; but they were not social revolutionaries, and their anxiety about the miners should have counted for more than it did with the Archbishop. It is not entirely surprising that the miners' leaders should have spoken of dealing with 'the representatives of the Christian Church'. (The absence of Roman Catholics was inevitable after the withdrawal from Copec.) Church historians tend to agree that not enough was done and to blame William Temple for not doing it, but Davidson's reduction of Anglican policy to his own 'high political' conversations in Westminster must bear some responsibility.

Frustration, therefore, partly explains the Standing Conference's unsuccessful effort at mediation in July. On 16 July Kirk wrote to Davidson, telling him that on 8 July the Conference had started by meeting representatives of the mine-owners, who had rejected suggestions made to them on the basis of the Samuel Report. Nevertheless, on 14 July the Conference had seen the miners' leaders, Smith, Cook and Richardson, and on the same basis had put together what was not a proposal for a settlement of the dispute, but a proposal that conditions for a settlement be set up, with the financial help of government. Kirk told Davidson that the Standing Conference had now asked for an interview with the Prime Minister. This meeting took place on 19 July, but before he met them, Baldwin published and rejected their proposals. Temple was one of five Conference speakers at the interview, and in a letter to his wife written on the same day he said that Baldwin 'attributes the perpetual trouble with coal to past readiness of Governments to intervene; he says the industry has been taught to expect public money whenever it howls and has determined to end that ... Plainly the Government wish that we would keep out of it, and are disposed to say that if we encourage the Miners we prolong the strike. They expect a break fairly soon. But that is a "war attitude" and is, I am sure, not the most right.'

Temple added that his 'one fright' had come afterwards when Kirk argued that if there was no concession from either government or owners the Standing Conference should be prepared to fight on the miners' side. Temple and Kempthorne resisted this, saying that in industrial conflicts the 'church' could mediate but not take sides. Temple commented to his wife: 'Cook, of course, will call us rats if we do not fight, and perhaps will be right to do so, but we must stick to our own job.' In effect, Temple and Kempthorne were saying that the coal dispute was not about broad changes of policy – that issue had been settled in the General Strike – but about local technical matters over which the church, as they conceived it, could not fight. Their position underlined the ambiguity inherent in claiming that 'the church' should have a social programme but should neither become nor foster a political organisation to promote it. When in the desperation of 1926 Kirk was talking as though this political force existed, the bishops were justified in disagreeing with him. Years later, in answering Seebohm Rowntree's complaint that the Standing Conference's public intervention had, by leading the miners to suppose that they had the whole of the Christian church behind them, wrecked the chance that a private initiative of Rowntree's might have ended the strike, Temple admitted that there had been 'a tendency to try to make capital for the Church out of it by publicity when the thing ought, if done at all, to have been kept entirely private' (8 July 1942, Iremonger, 1948, p. 342). The public intervention, however, stemmed from the late Victorian ecclesiastical tradition that bishops ought to act as umpires in industrial conflicts, a tradition which again implied that the 'church' could exercise political influence without responsibility.

Whether Kirk felt as put down about all this as later commentators have suggested is not clear. A few days later (23 July) he sent Davidson a copy of a 'Manifesto' which the Standing Conference was about to publish, which expressed more than sympathy with the miners' plight. It said that the Conference (which was already being attacked by parsons in *The Times* for interfering in secular affairs on the strength of sentimental Christian socialism) had laid before the government proposals which, in their view, should be accepted by all parties as a basis for resuming negotiations, 'but regrettably, as it seems to us, they do not secure the approval of the Prime Minister'. There must, nevertheless, be adequate pay and humane conditions of work. 'It is primarily to the spiritual and moral aspects of the crisis that we feel impelled to direct the attention of our fellow-Christians . . . large numbers of the miners and their families are enduring real privation . . . The temper of mutual trust, forbearance and good will which should be the note of a Christian society is gravely impaired. Moral considerations are weakened, and the spirit of assertion and domination finds expression in the demand sometimes thoughtlessly uttered for a "fight to a finish" . . . Such a spirit is anti-christian, and such utterances, from whomsoever they may proceed, are to be condemned by all Christian people.'

Davidson's response to this was scathing. He told Kempthorne (9 August 1926) that the Standing Conference's involvement was doing nothing but harm. Any further government money was now 'an anathema in the view of almost everybody'. There was no point in suggesting a four-month period for further discussion – a few days would do between men of goodwill. The full responsibility for the latest proposals should be placed on the miners, 'not on the shoulders of what is rather absurdly called the Church Party . . . What I dread . . . is that in a short time we shall find it stated that the arrayed forces consist of the Church plus the miners on one side and the government on the other side . . . a hopelessly unreasonable statement . . . I honestly think the government, or at least the Prime Minister, has acted with perfectly good faith throughout . . . and though there have I think been some mistakes I do not find it difficult to defend Baldwin's position' (Davidson Papers, vol. 273). Davidson offered no approval whatever to the Standing Conference; he wanted the issue closed.

Replying on 10 August 1926 Kempthorne was able to offer the withdrawal which the Archbishop so passionately wanted. The miners' leaders had put the proposals to their Districts, which had turned them down and so released everyone from a hopeless negotiation. Together with Temple, Edward Woods and three other bishops, Kempthorne had met the miners' leaders that afternoon: 'they are evidently disappointed'. There was no further question of 'fighting' on the miners' side, however, and Kempthorne recognised this by going to Switzerland on holiday. This was a retreat under fire, for by this time the barrage in The Times had reached the point where a correspondent asserted that 'a few bishops have been decoyed into the Communist trap' (11 August 1926).

Temple offered his own defence of the Standing Conference in The Times on 19 August. He accepted that ecclesiastics had no special insight into industrial disputes, but argued that the Standing Conference had not tried to produce proposals of its own but had simply tried to bring the miners and their opponents back to the Samuel Report as a basis for negotiation. By pointing out that Baldwin 'took the unusual step of publishing the suggested terms together with the Government's determination not to renew the subsidy before receiving our deputation', he underlined how determined the Prime Minister was that the churches should not even appear to define the moral context of industrial policy. Baldwin was quite serious when he said that the churches had no more business to try to settle the coal dispute than the Federation of British Industry had to seek revision of the Athanasian Creed, a remark that still rankled with Temple when he wrote Christianity and Social Order during the Second World War. Baldwin accepted the English post-seventeenth-century view that religious certainties poison politics. He himself did not want to change British society but to reconcile the nation as a whole to the existing system: the miners were a special case, and they had to be brought to heel. In the summer of 1926 Temple was so disturbed by the meagre results of the churches' intervention that he fell back on saying that the Standing Conference 'felt a responsibility for trying to secure that the settlement should be not only economically sound in itself, but reached with the minimum of bitterness or resentment and the maximum of good will'.

This sounded a little like Baldwin's position, and underlined the widespread anxiety which was felt about the cohesion of postwar British society, but the reference to 'economic soundness' was there as an escape clause, pointing back to Temple's willingness to change the balance of power, if he could find the leverage.

There are firm opinions about the significance for the churches of the General Strike and the subsequent mining strike. Professor Hastings, for example, thinks that 'the church' should have committed itself to the side of the miners after the failure of the Standing Conference's intervention in July 1926, and that it was Temple, obsessed with the church's role as a reconciler, who principally blocked the way. 'The failure of the churches to do anything significant in the strike, beyond Davidson's interim proposal, coming as it did just two years after all the fanfare of Copec showed only too revealingly the latter's weakness' (Hastings, 1986, p. 192). Dr Norman is just as trenchant: public reaction to episcopal intervention was to reject the 'claim of the Church to be the Minister of reconciliation', and Norman concludes that 'Church social radicalism had developed in isolation from realities – in episcopal palaces, in study groups and Conferences, in Theological Colleges and University common-rooms. In 1926 the door had been opened and a very cold blast had withered the hothouse growths. The Church's passion for social criticism survived the experience, but its growth was stunted' (Norman, 1976, p. 340). A. M. Suggate thinks that the strikes showed that Copec was naive about the empirical difficulties of translating its ideal social targets into reality. His own view was that 'over most issues, because of their complexity, it will be best to implement the dialectical method by setting up an inquiry which draws on first-hand experience and the perspectives of various disciplines and aims at a report which is thoroughly empirical as well as theological' (Suggate, 1987, pp. 146–50). It is arguable, however, that in the 1926 coal disputes there was a plethora of empirical enquiry, and that the weakness of the approach of Temple and others lay neither in theology nor in their knowledge of the empirical facts, but in their trying to influence political conflict when they themselves had so little political power on which to draw.

Norman says that Hensley Henson was nearer to the mind of the ordinary Englishman than Temple, which would imply that further action would have been a waste of time and that further enquiry would have led away from social radicalism. Temple could reasonably have replied that in July 1926 intervention was no longer about complicated constitutional or economic issues but was aimed, over-optimistically, at extricating the miners from a battle they could not win. All three scholars rather neglect the point that all the Anglican bishops involved in the Standing Conference were well aware that Davidson was totally opposed to what they were doing, and that there was no practical hope of committing Anglicanism on the miners' side. They had no compensatory political organisation: Kirk was far from being a major figure in 1926, the ICF was more of a revivalist than a socialist mission, and the Copec Continuation Committee, of which Charles Raven was the ineffective secretary, showed itself to be a feeble pressure-group. Their greatest mistake was in supposing that they could deal with the Prime Minister, who may or may not have been what Henson called him, 'a Christian statesman', but who was certainly more than a match politically for the would-be mediators. He had cut the Archbishop of Canterbury out of the General Strike, and now he eliminated 'the church' from the miners' strike. Both then and in the 1930s Baldwin outmanoeuvred neo-Anglicans like Temple – anxious to strengthen the state church by giving it a stake in the national soul – by presenting himself and the Conservative Party as the custodians of 'English' national unity: politics, not religion, was to be the source of the common faith and the binding set of values. The national soul was safe in Conservative hands.

Logically, those who thought that the national soul was safer in Anglican keeping should have formed a religious political party and taken the consequences of electoral insignificance which were almost inevitable without proportional representation. In some European countries the Catholic laity persuaded the Vatican to tolerate a political party organised on a Catholic basis. In Britain, Nonconformity had briefly solved the political problem by identifying itself with the Liberal Party and had even, about 1900, begun to think of the Liberal Party as an extension of Nonconformity, but the experiment collapsed with the decline of both Liberalism and the Free churches. There was no possibility of identifying the Copec programme with interwar Conservatism, and the 1927 Trade Disputes Act showed how little political influence religious radicalism had as against the growing conviction of the twentieth-century Tory Party that unions were becoming an undesirable extension of working-class power. Towards the end of his career Temple felt closer to the Labour Party than to the Conservatives, but in 1926 he seemed to see all three parties as united in a rejection of the organic Christian society which for him was the will of God. The difference between his position and that of late Victorian Nonconformity was that while Nonconformity had been driven by social discrimination to accept a conflict model of British society from which political action naturally followed, Temple, on the other hand, hoped that Anglicanism could express and even incorporate the essential unity of British society.

Such a combination of religion and politics had briefly seemed possible in Edwardian England. Ever since the 1880s 'advanced Liberals' had lived off a secular enthusiasm for the idea that the universe itself was both dynamic and progressive, gradual and continuous. This meant that politically the alternative to past corruption was not revolution, but a new version of natural 'law' which expressed itself through 'development' instead of through the rigidities of the Newtonian and Manchester School systems. This was a universe in which 'God' could survive because order would be preserved and yet development would take place. This world-view suited many different people, because some found it ethically adequate without Christian dogma to support it, while Christian theologians could easily, if illogically, add dogma (the Incarnation, the atonement, the Resurrection of Christ and so forth) to the secular system. William Temple did so himself when he assumed that, however one described the Christian God's party membership, the universe was certainly on the side of universal rather than selective benefits: full employment, good housing, popular education and some kind of national medical system. The crisis of 1926 revealed how far the social basis of this outlook had collapsed, at least for the time being, so that the battle of ideas, in which middle-class intellectuals like Temple were often brilliant and persuasive, had given way to a battle in terms of social power and physical force. 'Labour' refused to accept the New Liberal policy of a common advance towards a common felicity, industry was not prepared to yield to metaphysics, and some even of the Left-Liberals reacted to the General Strike by calling for social compulsion, not persuasion. J. A. Hobson, for example, said that the strikes pointed to the need for some conscious regulation of the industrial system in terms of its social or organic unity. He thought that the absolute right to strike had to go, and deplored the trade union tendency to act in terms of free-market bargaining (Hobson, 1927). Temple also found that his close friend Tawney, who was as convinced a Christian as he was himself, accepted a conflict model of society and firmly supported the General Strike and the miners' strike.

At this stage, then, Temple's career changed gear. There was no question of personal failure – he was prominent at the Lausanne Faith and Order Conference in 1927 and at the Jerusalem Missionary Council in 1928 – but the direction had changed: he had sidestepped the impasse of religion and politics and moved to the specialist area of ecumenism, where he tried to create more powerful religious institutions. In 1929 he became the chairman of the Continuation Committee of Faith and Order and Archbishop of York – he was forty-eight and fully incorporated into the religious Establishment.

## THE MALVERN CONFERENCE 1941

In the 1920s and 1930s most Christian leaders, including Temple, assumed that the contemporary church (however identified) was at the spiritual and political centre of human history, and that no kind of significant progress was sustainable without it. Both Catholic and Protestant theologians looked at contemporary history from the ecclesia outwards, resented (when they did not reject) the Enlightenment and often harked back to periods like the high Middle Ages, when the Western church seemed to them to have had its proper place in Western culture. They also approved of the expanding part which Christian missions had taken in the European penetration of the heartlands of other world religions. It must, they believed, be the will of the Christian God that a church-based culture should occupy the whole world; this was why they attached such importance to the ecumenical movement. Temple grew up under the influence of the earlier, more sanguine version of this outlook, when the British Empire still seemed the model of an attainable future. When the events of the 1920s and 1930s made these theologians pessimistic about the future, they sometimes fell back on what they called 'eschatology': the dogmatic assertion that in the long run – perhaps at the 'end' of history – God would intervene to ensure the 'church's' triumph. This was not, as has often been claimed by orthodox church historians who prefer Karl Barth and Reinhold Niebuhr to William Temple, the development of a deeper insight into Christian theology, but a retreat to ecclesiastical fastnesses from which it was difficult to communicate with the outside world at all. Politically, the church-centred sub-culture of the 1930s in Britain was diverse: it included the Anglo-Catholic Christendom Group, for instance, which looked down on practical politics; the Moot, which was more interested in power than theology, and whose members believed that a handful of Christian intellectuals could permeate and control society in the style of the Webbs; and those Roman Catholics for whom General Franco had become a defender of 'Christian civilisation' and for whom contemporary history had become a struggle between 'the church' and Communism.

As for the small and unfashionable group of liberal or critical theologians, they increasingly doubted that one could maintain a view of the modern world which placed the Christian churches at the centre. They wanted greater doctrinal freedom inside the Christian sub-culture and were not hostile to humanism, whereas the church-centred sub-culture could not tolerate the idea of humanism as a serious alternative to Christianity. Temple differed from many of his Evangelical and Anglo-Catholic contemporaries in his will-ingness to tolerate liberal theology at an official level – in the 1938 report on doctrine, for example, which he signed and which they shelved – but both as an ecumenist and as a domestic politician part of his aim, nevertheless, was to make the Christian religion the base of society.

The position of the liberals was complicated in the 1930s by the question of pacifism, which in its absolute Christian form was a church-centred solution to the problems of political violence set by Communism and Fascism. Temple himself, like so many others, never abandoned the argument that the war-guilt clauses of the Versailles treaty were a mistake which partially justified German nationalism, but he dismissed pacifism as a serious political and religious option. Nevertheless, in the later 1930s he came nearer to the liberals, in the sense that he came to regard the achievement of the religiously neutral social planning embodied in the Malvern-Penguin programme in 1941/2 as more important theologically – I emphasise the paradox – than the church-centred conviction (which united Anglo-Catholics and Roman Catholics with many Evangelicals) that only through the 'church' could anything useful be done for sinful man and a sick society. In the later 1930s Temple's comparative isolation increased when Christians divided under the pressure of events, with the pacifists deploring conflict and the remainder responding in terms of whatever they felt to be the greatest menace: Marxism and Russia, the Fascist powers, or that vaguer common denominator, humanism. In its extreme form this reaction produced the kind of right-wing Roman Catholic who favoured an alliance between Britain and Hitler to destroy Russia.

Iremonger and other writers have said that four to five hundred people met at Malvern, but the real figure was about 210. They were not handpicked: the Conference was advertised, about 500 applied to come, and it was a question of first come, first served. Those who came all seem to have been Anglican, so this was not a repeat of Copec in 1924. As to political balance, the accuracy of E. R. Norman's complaint that 'the Right was not there' depends on one's definition of 'the right'. The Anglo-Catholic Christendom Group was heavily represented, for example, but however radical its members liked to think themselves, they were not socialist, and the mood and prejudices of their intellectual leader, V. A. Demant, resembled those of the more respectable part of the European Catholic Right, with its visceral reaction against the Enlightenment, the French Revolution and 'usury'. As recently as 1939 Demant, in *The Religious Prospect*, had vigorously denounced 'Liberalism' in all its forms, not excluding Liberal Protestantism. Another of the principal speakers at Malvern was the poet T. S. Eliot, who certainly belonged to the intellectual and romantic right, was a member of the Oldham-Mannheim 'Moot', to which Temple did not belong, and who contributed an essay on 'Cultural Forces in the Human Order' to Christendom's post-Malvern symposium, *Prospect for Christendom* (1945).

The Christendom Group, whose writers rarely mentioned Temple's social theology, would have liked to think itself traditional and unaffected by intellectual fashion (following fashion was a sin of liberals), but in practice it was very fashionable indeed in its open despair about the existing British political system. Many influences were at work here. There was an element of theological superiority, the conviction that a knowledge of Catholic dogma and the medieval social system was the divinely given key for solving modern economic problems. Contemporary writers also had their influence: the Anglo-Catholic monk J. N. Figgis, for example, whose *Churches in the Modern State* (1913) championed the rights of small social groups and associations against the centralising state; and the eccentric A. J. Penty, whose book *The Restoration of the Gild System* (1906) advocated a return to an organic medieval economy based on agriculture and handicrafts; while the Roman Catholic publicist, Hilaire Belloc, in *The Servile State* (1912), summed up in his title the view, popular in Christendom circles, that there was nothing to choose between socialist collectivism and social domination by a small, conspiratorial world of finance.

Belloc's ideas look like a romanticised, Catholic and anti-Semitic version of syndicalism, which had spread its influence far beyond its secular home in working-class politics. It sought, however, to find a basis for the individual worker's freedom in individual union-controlled factories, whereas Belloc, wholly anti-industrial, exalted the life of small peasant proprietors. The emotional difference between these overlapping positions and that of Temple may be summed up in a quotation from the ablest Guild Socialist writer, G. D. H. Cole, who wrote in 1917:

What, I want to ask, is the fundamental evil in our modern society which we should set out to abolish? There are two possible answers to the question, and I am sure that very many well-meaning people would make the wrong one. They would answer POVERTY, when they ought to answer SLAVERY. (Cole, 1917, p. 110)

Temple consistently regarded poverty and unemployment as fundamental evils which ought to be tackled without waiting for either the Kingdom of God or the syndicalist society. The Christendom Group put the need to make drastic changes in the basic structure of society first. Cole's priority had been to transfer political power to the industrial worker; Christendom wanted to restore Christian social hegemony on the economic basis of a radically less industrial society. Temple would not have been surprised that neither the secular Guild Socialists nor the 'catholic' Christendom Group achieved much in practice. He himself enjoyed abstract argument of this kind and delighted in defining 'principles', but when the debate was over, he always wanted to produce a list of clear practical demands which were not just the middle axioms which are often said to be his hallmark. The Malvern Conference would be no exception.

Christendom had taken a different path from Temple's after the end of the First World War. Over-alarmed by what were seen as the materialist and aggressive tactics of the larger trade unions, the group had broken with direct political action, rejected any contact with the Labour Party, and had committed itself as an Anglican pressure-group to working out what was usually called a 'Christian sociology'. What this meant was always vague, but in 1923 a Christendom manifesto attacked 'capitalist plutocracy and the wage system'; there was no comment on public ownership, but there was a new insistence on the centrality of Catholic dogma and medieval precedent to sound social thinking. Temple, on the other hand, had reacted to the rapidly changing postwar situation by organising the Copec Conference in the hope of creating a socio-religious movement which would unite all the Christian churches. Christendom sought to distinguish itself from both untheological socialism and non-revolutionary Christianity. By the time that the members had started *Christendom: a Journal of Christian Sociology* in 1931, they had wrecked their economic reputation by committing themselves to Social Credit, a case of one small sect falling under the spell of another small sect. Only a short time before the Malvern Conference Demant had said that true spiritual revolution meant abandoning the fetish of industrialism and returning to 'economic realism by giving priority to the earth over commerce and money' (Demant, 1939, p. 241).

What linked Temple to the members of the Christendom Group in spite of these disagreements was that both they and Temple thought that a genuine solution to the economic problems of the early twentieth century had to be based on a

Christian theology; but whereas Temple realised that any proposed theological reconstruction of Western industrial society in the 1920s had to accept the creative, expansionist side of capitalism, they reacted against the modern economic system as part of a wider Western betrayal of true Christianity. Their standard of an ideal Christian society was medieval Catholic Europe: only if the church could once again incorporate the whole world into itself would they be satisfied, and they could imagine this incorporation only in terms of a return to medieval social order, complete with a guild system of production and the theory of the just price. They were utopian revolutionaries of the right rather than the left, but a theory of permanently unattainable revolution is likely to fade gradually into a state of permanent hopelessness, or, as happened sometimes in this case, into a state of dilettante disdain. There was a dubious sound about the constant emphasis on the evils of 'capitalist plutocracy': once more one is reminded of the sophisticated anti-Semitism of the extreme Catholic right. In international affairs, for example, Christendom writers could dismiss the League of Nations as 'an instrument of centralised and secretive finance'. Such a comment suggested that the benefits of Catholic dogma did not save the Christendom Group from other not-so-secret obsessions which prevented it from making any serious assessment of the practical possibilities of the League's tenuous existence.

From Temple's point of view it was unfortunate that even as late as the early 1940s the principal group of Anglican intellectuals who were thinking about social questions should have been so hostile to his basic approach. It was all very well, for example, for those who belonged to the Christendom Group to take an ascetic view of economics, no doubt closely related to their medievalism, but this meant that they too easily despised the modern combination of scientific innovation and large-scale production; instead, they fussed in a recognisably secular way about the dangers to spiritual progress in a system in which more and more people might possess a car, a telephone and a radio. There was something equally insensitive about their passionate disapproval of birth control, which Temple did not share. Nevertheless, Temple accepted them as allies in so far as they were genuinely concerned about poverty, unemployment and cultural deprivation.

As Archbishop of York, Temple did not have the time in 1941 to organise the Malvern Conference himself: this was done by his longterm associate P. T. R. Kirk, through his organisation, the Industrial Christian Fellowship, which also saw to the publication of Malvern documents in the following months. The stated object of the Conference 'was to consider from the Anglican point of view what are the fundamental facts which are directly relevant to the ordering of the new society that is quite evidently emerging, and how Christian thought can be shaped to play a leading part in the reconstruction after the war is over'. The leaders of Christendom, people like Demant and Reckitt, did not fully sympathise with what Temple meant in saying that a 'new society' was quite evidently emerging. They were not interested in how the secular society was likely to change, because they felt that it could only change for the worse; they came to Malvern chiefly concerned to advocate their own view of a divinely ordered society on a medieval model. Temple, on the other hand, believed – and this time he was nearer to the truth than he had been in 1917/18 – that once again war was about to provide the chance of social reconstruction, and he knew from his own experience how bitterly that chance had been dissipated between 1918 and 1926. He desperately wanted the Church of England to be more efficiently prepared for social action once the war had been won than it had been before then. That was why, although he sympathised with Christendom's talk about a divinely appointed social order which sinful humanity had abandoned for an unnatural order of their own, he was more concerned to use the Malvern Conference as the start of a campaign for less abstract ideas. This was the motive which Corelli Barnett, in *The Audit of War* (1986), regarded as part of a wartime Christian conspiracy to make the idea of a welfare state the centre of postwar British policy when what really mattered was industrial and financial reconstruction. Demant and his colleagues came to Malvern expecting discussion which they would dominate; instead, they found Temple anxious to pave the way for specific action, together with other Anglicans who seemed to be reviving the 'socialism' from which Christendom had broken away.

These differences, and the context of a desperate war which had not yet by any means been won, explain why the Malvern Conference was not like the elated, almost too harmonious Copec of nearly twenty years before. As soon as the Conference was finished, Demant and Hodges (who was Professor of Philosophy at Reading, a regular attender at the Moot, and sympathetic to Mannheim's search for a 'third way' between Fascism and Communism) complained to Temple that they had expected close discussion in a group of about forty people, a kind of extension of the Moot itself, which often discussed the possibility of a small Christian lay order which would quietly penetrate the centres of power. Instead, Hodges said, he had found himself addressing a mass meeting consisting partly of currency reformers and partly of socialists, the whole being in his opinion 'incompetent'. This idea of Malvern's 'incompetence', which also appeared in a letter from A. R. Vidler to Temple (14 January 1941), has been frequently repeated, though there is no evidence that the Conference differed much from other ecclesiastical meetings as far as competence is concerned.

At Malvern itself, where the Conference was held between 7 and 10 January 1941, the main battleground turned out to be a left-wing resolution proposed by two Anglican laymen, Sir Richard Acland, a professional cross-bench politician with radical leanings, and Kenneth Ingram, who in 1937 had published a book called *Christianity – Right or Left?*, in which he argued that the churches had no alternative but to choose the hard left in the struggle between Communism and Fascism. In the programme they were supposed to be talking about 'Practical Questions', and their resolution cut through the highminded vagueness of the Christendom Group (whose speakers dealt with 'The Basic Problem of Contemporary Society' and 'Economics') and attacked as contrary to divine justice the notion of private property, and specifically the private ownership of the principal industrial resources of the community. After the Conference, Demant spent until early May trying to prevent the publication of his own paper in the same volume as the addresses of Acland and Ingram, on the ground that this would give the impression that he agreed that 'the sting of our capitalist evil lies in this form of property', i.e. the private ownership of industrial assets (28 April 1941, Demant to Kirk, in Temple Papers, vol. 33).

If this resolution had been accepted in its original form, it would have implied that some prominent Anglicans thought that private property and Christianity were incompatible, placing people like Temple, as Archbishop of York, in apparent public opposition to the Conservative Party, a situation which seemed rational to Acland. The Bishop of Chichester, George Bell, who with Temple's encouragement had made himself an expert on unemployment during the 1930s, moved an amendment which seems to have been carried by 75 votes to 60, a total vote which offers additional confirmation of the actual scale of the Conference. Bell's amendment stopped short of a Christian condemnation of all private property, but attacked those forms of it which produced deprivation among the poor. The closeness of the voting explains why Acland and Bell then spent some time in arranging an agreed resolution between them.

The final wording was carried without votes against, but at least some of the Christendom Group abstained, and Temple's correspondence, now at Lambeth Palace, shows that Demant, Eliot, Hodges and Vidler did not agree with the resolution. It did not commit the Conference to opposing private property as such, but rather to the belief

that the maintenance of that part of the structure of our society, by which the *ultimate* ownership of the principal industrial resources of the community can be vested in the hands of private owners, *may be* ... a stumbling block ... contrary to divine justice, making it harder for men to live Christian lives. On the one hand it may deprive the poorest members of the community of the essentials of life. On the other, while these resources can be so owned, men will strive for their ownership for themselves. As a consequence, a way of life founded on the supremacy of the economic motive will remain, which is contrary to God's plan for mankind. (my italics)

Christians should strive towards a form of society in which, while the essential value of the human personality was preserved, the continuance of these abuses would no longer be possible.

Temple wrote to Acland in February 1941:

When your first resolution was carried I was rather embarrassed because it would have been quite necessary that in publishing it I should have made quite clear my own dissent and I expect that would have been true of many other people in the minority who had special official responsibilities. Certainly, some of the bishops present voted against it as did all the members, as far as I could see, of the Christendom group . . . Then the bishop of Chichester

produced his amendment which was carried by a narrow majority
... This was in itself of course a great relief ... Then you generously
proposed that you and the bishop should see if you could produce
an agreed form. You were successful in this.

I slightly regret the change from 'is' to 'may be' at the beginning
of the controversial clause of the resolution. That did seem to me
rather to draw the sting of anything that it might contain but I dare
say the Conference could not have agreed to it if the word 'is' had
remained. But to me the introduction of the word 'ultimate' made
all the difference.

You objected to our argument that communal ownership will
work out in a tyrannous bureaucratic control on the ground that we
must not desert the right principle because it may be abused. On the
other hand, I maintain that a certain amount of effective private
property, which must, I think, extend beyond a man's house and
garden, is part of the sound principle ... I quite definitely think the
system in Russia, as far as I know anything about it, much worse
than our own.

Temple described the traditional Christian doctrine of
property, about which Acland had enquired, as 'a full
recognition of private property combined with an insistence
that it must always carry responsibility. The property without
function is the thing that is condemned. Now this condemns
a very large amount of the property which exists today: to
some extent in land, to an enormous extent in stocks and
shares.'

Temple concluded:

The main concern of most people with the right of investment is
not to make a fortune but to obtain a modest security and I believe
that this is spiritually healthy. Most people can only reach spiritual
freedom if they are to some extent economically secure ... I think
the position of the ordinary debenture holder is morally sound and
socially valuable. (7 February 1941, Temple Papers, vol. 33)

Acland (writing on 3 February 1941) had been confident
that the day of large-scale private enterprise was finished:

'There is now among politicians, no dispute whatever that we cannot go on with each private owner having an absolute right to do just exactly what he likes with his own. This is universally accepted except among a few pathetically isolated little groups of laisser-faireists who have no influence at all.' Acland's evidence for this assertion would probably have been the British wartime consensus that victory over Nazi Germany required a command economy, but what the Malvern resolution referred to was the postwar world, and there Acland was unrealistic as far as the hard core of the Conservative Party was concerned. On the other hand, it is also true that the post-1945 nationalisation of major industries like coal and transport and the setting-up of the National Health Service were received with remarkable equanimity by the general community.

The language of the Acland–Bell form of the resolution may seem at first sight to echo the ideas of *Christianity and Industrial Problems*, the famous Anglican report of 1918, which had argued that cooperation for public service rather than competition for private gain should be the guiding-line of a Christian economy. A second reading suggests a moralistic compromise which was not intended to justify 'socialist' conclusions. It is not surprising that Temple should have told Acland that he regretted the change from 'is' to the damp moderation of 'may be', but he approved of the insertion of 'ultimate' (which seemed weak to Acland, though he had accepted it in the Conference) because the question what kind of final authority, if any, society possessed over the basic industries was vital, outweighing argument for and against specific schemes of nationalisation.

Some of the Christendom Group abstained in the final vote on the resolution. This was no doubt because they held that private property and the family were the foundations of a Christian free society. Presumably others – A. R. Vidler, for example, who despite his worries about the 'competence' of his fellow delegates had failed to make his objections to the Conference's conclusions clear at the time – also abstained. The published version seems to have been sharper than Bell's version, which did not say that the 'economic motive' was contrary to God's plan for mankind. According to Temple, Demant's objection to Acland and Ingram's resolution was that undiluted socialism would lead to totalitarianism of a bureaucratic kind. This was a longstanding Catholic objection at the theoretical level to the Welfare State, and one which Temple shared to some extent, without concluding that the positive state could only exist in an oppressively bureaucratic form.

As far as the Church of England was concerned, Malvern undoubtedly expressed a resurgence of the more radical Anglican attitudes to unemployment and poverty which had dropped into the background after 1926. The economic collapse of 1929–31 and the rapid advance of Nazism and Fascism were chiefly responsible for the change. Ingram and Acland had little solid support in Anglicanism for their attack on private property, but Temple's conviction, as Archbishop of York, that there must be new social limits on the freedom of private capitalism gave their ideas more resonance in ecclesiastical circles. Bell's presence at Malvern was not mentioned by either Iremonger or E. R. Norman, and is missing from his official biography as well. Yet it was important, because his role in the Conference underlines the fact that it was not a case of Temple's imposing his own views on the Church of England through a packed meeting. Bell was no simple and obedient follower: he was a serious candidate for Canterbury until his opposition to the wartime aerial bombardment of Germany isolated him politically. It was significant that so independent a bishop was following a line close to Temple's. Temple himself was not committed to 'socialism' in Acland's sense. He did not think that the Christian churches faced an either/or choice between Communism and Fascism, as Ingram believed, nor did he think that the theologian, in looking for a seriously Christian alternative to these political messianisms, was obliged to turn to the Christendom Group's idealised medievalism.

What Demant, Eliot, Hodges and Vidler disliked about Malvern was the shift from the kind of conference which discussed papers and went away marvelling at its own contradictions, to a conference which issued public statements about how the national economy ought to be run as the considered conclusions of a significant body of religious people headed by the Archbishop of York, himself no minor figure in the Church of England. Temple, whose wider intentions should never have been in doubt among people many of whom had known him for years, tried to meet criticism of the way in which he exploited the Conference by arguing that the Anglican church ought to be thinking aloud about social questions in view of the crisis which would follow the winning of the war.

The counter view, that the Conference had exceeded its brief and was 'incompetent', was tantamount to admitting that the Anglican church had nothing to say about these matters: after all, most of those Anglicans who habitually wrote on social subjects were there, and the Moot was represented as well as Christendom. Whether Christendom itself was 'competent' was a different question, although the group's Social Credit aberration does not seem to have played an important part at Malvern. Temple could play on its rather elitist contempt for capitalism, but he could not expect it to give whole-hearted support to the detailed programme which he attached to Malvern. Temple was bound to take for granted the indifference of those on the Evangelical right,

who broadly held that the Christian gospel was a message of
individual spiritual regeneration, not social reform. He was
anxious only to avoid provoking their hostility by seeming to
move too close to the secular political left.

As for the Moot's political position (which touched
Malvern directly through Eliot, Hodges and Vidler), José
Harris has drawn attention to a programme for the reform of
the postwar educational system drawn up for R. A. Butler as
Education Secretary in 1942 by a Christian group which drew
many of its practical ideas from the Moot's central figure, Karl
Mannheim. 'This group set out a programme . . . based on
state take-over of the public schools, compulsory technical
and vocational training for all 14–18 year olds, conscription
of youth into organised youth movements, the replacement
of classics by a national curriculum of science and techno-
logy, and the inculcation of public spirit through the
teaching of Christian doctrine' (Harris, 1990, p. 192). The
total rejection of this scheme by the Conservative Party's
Central Council in September 1942 (as, among other things,
'Christian fascism') drew a line beyond which Temple could
not go in the negotiations which preceded the 1944
Education Act.

Temple summed up his impressions of what had happened
at Malvern in a revealing letter to Kirk of 21 February 1941, in
which he said that he was afraid that

the movement may get into the hands, through inadvertence, of
Anglo-Catholics and that therefore the Evangelical school will be
too little represented and perhaps placed in something like
opposition . . . [or] that it will get into the hands of the political left
and therefore alienate a large section of both Anglo-Catholics and
Evangelicals.

If Ingram, who was more of a left-wing extremist than
Acland, emerged as the chief spokesman,

we shall lose entirely the Christendom group, with whom I am personally in much closer agreement than with Acland and Ingram. It would simply be felt that we had 'gone left', and while in actual policy I imagine all of us have much more sympathy with the Left than with the greater portion of the Right wing, we must be very careful that we do not give the impression that the Church is an agency for supporting Left-Wing policies, which are often based on presuppositions which are completely unChristian. (Temple Papers, vol. 33)

Iremonger did not print this letter, and E. R. Norman quoted only from the latter part, starting from 'we must be very careful': he inadvertently printed 'politics' instead of 'policies', and left the impression that the letter might have been written before Malvern, instead of after.

On 26 June 1941 Kirk informed Temple that the Industrial Christian Fellowship had issued nearly 200,000 copies of a brief summary of the conclusions of Malvern; by 28 February 1942 he was reporting the sale of 30,000 copies of a sixteen-page pamphlet, *Malvern and After*, which Temple had drafted. These figures make the later sale of 140,000 copies of Temple's Penguin Special, *Christianity and Social Order*, less surprising: some Penguin Specials, however, sold about twice this number; the Left Book Club had 57,000 members in 1939 and perhaps three times that many readers (Mills and Smith, 1987, p. 199). Both Kirk and Temple wanted a movement – Temple was already using the word 'movement' in the February 1941 letter just quoted – and Kirk was also pleading for two-day conventions in the larger cities of England and Wales, with Temple as chairman. Both wanted to prevent the Malvern initiative from petering out in the way that Copec had done.

Temple now summarised the Malvern statement in a paper dated 25–7 July 1941, with the idea of holding further meetings in London with a small hand-picked group. He offered six objectives for discussion. These were as follows:

1 'Every child should find itself a member of a family housed with decency and dignity . . .'

2 'Every child should have the opportunity of an education till years of maturity . . . this education should throughout be inspired by faith in God and find its focus in worship . . .'

3 Families should have an income which would make these first two points possible.

4 'Every individual should have a voice in the control of the business which is carried on by means of his labour.'

5 'Sufficient daily leisure, with the weekly day of rest, and annual holiday with pay, to enable him to enjoy a full personal life'.

6 Freedom of worship, speech, assembly, etc.

In the form given above, this list of objectives appeared in *Malvern and After*, which the ICF published in the autumn of 1941, and they formed, without material alteration, the most important section of the Penguin Special, whose preface was dated 15 November 1941, though publication was in 1942. These links and sales figures suggest that E. R. Norman was on the wrong tack when he wrote that 'Temple's last great contribution to the social Christianity he had done so much to foster was not the Malvern Conference – it was the publication of his Penguin Special in 1942' (Norman, 1976, p. 367). These activities were related, not distinct. In view of the role which the Christendom Group had played at Malvern, it is also interesting that these objectives were not a summary of what it wanted: Christendom was opposed to any expansion of state welfare activity on the ground that a society which took what might be regarded as secular welfare for granted would be less likely to respond to a dogmatic Christian form of social action.

Instead, Temple was accepting advice from J. M. Keynes,

an economist with a New Liberal background who had no interest in Christianity at all, but who saw no reason why the Church of England should not intervene in socio-economic fields. Keynes encouraged Temple in the direction of a mixed economy: on the question of banks, for example, he wrote that if the Malvern document meant

the nationalisation of the Big Five Banks, I should prefer the methods of control by which their profit-earning possibilities were limited and they became to a great extent agents of the State without divesting them of their separate personalities and systems of control. Generally speaking, I prefer mixed systems for the future which lie somewhere between nationalisation in the old sense and private enterprise in the old sense. (28 October 1941, Temple Papers, vol. 33)

The Malvern Conference had not, however, fulfilled the hopes which Temple had of it, and it is true that his attachment of the Conference's 'authority' to his own preferred social policy looks a little cavalier. But he shared with most of the delegates a dislike for what has been called a 'two-thirds society', one in which a large majority of the population enjoy security of employment and draw a comfortable income, banishing from their imagination and from politics the existence of a marginalised minority. Many writers have been anxious to show that by the late 1930s Temple was moving away from the Hegelian optimism of his early theology and coming closer to the neo-orthodox pessimism which they themselves prefer (Suggate, 1987, for example).

On the contrary, Temple's willingness after Malvern to make yet another major attempt to influence national political life, a decision which committed him to considerable editorial work and correspondence, to writing the Penguin Special and to touring the country chairing meetings and making speeches, all in addition to his normal burden as an Archbishop and ended only by his death, witnesses to his strong belief that Anglicanism must discharge its role as the established form of Christianity in England by bringing pressure to bear on the state in favour of specific social changes.

*Chapter 4*

# A reassessment

In Temple's lifetime the question of establishment was discussed by two internal Anglican committees; these produced the Selborne Report in 1917 and the Cecil Report of 1935; Temple took part in both committees. These reports, when taken together with two later enquiries, the Moberley (1952) and the Chadwick (1970), suggest a gently rising recovery of Anglican satisfaction with establishment as such, side by side with a growing conviction that modernisation required the Church of England to be 'spiritually independent'. This status was usually defined as Davidson had defined it in the 1920s, as the freedom of the church to arrange its own worship and define its own doctrinal position without any amendment by Parliament, while retaining a social primacy over other churches which was expressed in 1970 in the claim that 'the historic relationship of Church and people in England is still alive, if only as a sentiment inhibiting change' (Chadwick, 1970, p. 72). At the end of the First World War many Anglicans imagined that spiritual independence had been effectively created through the machinery of the Church Assembly, but this was not the case, as the parliamentary rejection of the Prayer Book Measure in 1928 and 1929 had clearly shown. Politicians, for whom modernisation in this case meant the elimination of

Anglicanism from everyday political business as far as possible, accepted the Enabling Act and the later modifications which replaced the Assembly with the General Synod in 1970 as steps in the right direction, but as long as the established church implied that it was also 'the Church of the English people', neither spiritual nor political independence was likely to be fully conceded. In practice, there was an underlying implication, in line with Davidson's views, not Temple's, that in return for greater authority over matters of doctrine and worship the Church of England would leave politics to the politicians. The effort to sustain an Anglican political pressure-group, never strong after 1945, had broken down by the end of the 1960s. The most important benefit of the degree of modernisation which was achieved was that the formal presence of the laity as part of the government of the church made it easier for the whole body to accept the idea of ordaining women to the Anglican priesthood, though it is significant that no woman had actually been ordained by 1990. The mills of the Anglican God were grinding as slowly as ever.

Temple would not have been overimpressed by what had been achieved. It was true that the 1917 report had led to the setting-up of the Church Assembly, but the new institution did not reduce the tension between Anglican Evangelicals, Liberals and Anglo-Catholics, or between church and state, and it did not release fresh Anglican energies. What Temple and his more radical supporters, such as Albert Mansbridge of the WEA, had originally hoped for was to be found in an appendix to the Selborne Report on the relationship between the working classes and the Church of England. Here it was admitted that hostility existed between the working classes and the Establishment, and that this sprang partly from their feeling that the Anglican church was a policeman which the propertied groups used to protect themselves, and partly from a proletarian belief that the moral teaching of the church opposed social change (Selborne, 1917, p. 253). 'How can religion', the appendix asked, 'from a force acting on individuals as it were privately become more of a force acting on them in their social relations also?' (p. 250). This was precisely the question which Temple kept on asking all his life, but there was no answer in Selborne. On a practical level, there was a plea for working-class priests (though not much idea how to find them), and a proposal that each Diocesan Conference should select a small group of 'wage-earners' to take part in the election of the new House of Laymen which was a fundamental part of the proposed Church Assembly. Significantly, this last idea was not taken up. It was only in a few passages like this, however, that the 1917 report showed any trace of Temple's desire to convert the Church of England from a comfortable and comforting partner of government into a body which would feel free to act as a social critic. His suspicion that Archbishop Davidson was manipulating the wartime reform movement in order to prevent any such outcome explains the fury with which he occasionally attacked the episcopal leadership during the Life and Liberty campaign.

The Cecil Report (1935) was limited by its origins in the pseudo-crisis created in the Church of England by Parliament's rejection, in 1927/8, of the Church Assembly's proposed revision of the Prayer Book. The crisis underlined the extent to which Davidson had failed to obtain 'spiritual independence' in 1919, and how he had deceived himself about his ability to manage the world of high politics. But the crisis was not really about the 'inalienable right of the Church to formulate its Faith and to arrange that Holy Faith in its forms of worship', to quote the resolution which Temple himself moved in February 1930 to set up the Cecil Committee (Church Assembly Proceedings, 1930, p. 60). The crisis occurred because Anglican Evangelicals and Anglo-Catholics would not agree how the Church of England should arrange its form of worship, and the Cecil Report's recommendation that there should be a Round Table Conference to secure agreement between the two sides was no more than a council of despair which failed in practice. When he was not ill Lang lacked energy, and Temple's alleged gift as a deviser of reconciling formulae worked no miracles here, either in the later 1930s or in 1943–4, when Bell urged Temple, now at Canterbury, to try again. On that occasion Temple found himself repeating the argument which Davidson had employed against him during the First World War, that the Prime Minister, now Winston Churchill instead of Lloyd George, could not safely be approached on such a subject in wartime (Jasper, 1967, pp. 190–3). He had, in any case, no influence with Churchill, who had no use either for Temple's 'socialism', or for his constant plea for a clearer definition of the Allies' war aims – Temple dismissed the 1941 Atlantic Charter as 'Victorian Liberalism' (F. S. Temple, 1963, p. 156). Temple could hardly claim that between 1919 and 1944 he had done much to change the way in which the establishment worked, and some people felt that living inside the system for many years had corrupted his judgement to the point that, like Lang, he was content to see the establishment last his time.

One example of such a hostile reaction was that of Temple's own biographer, F. A. Iremonger, writing in 1948, who, when he reached the question of church and state, abandoned his usual calm for vigorous criticism. 'His attitude towards the Establishment', Iremonger wrote, 'and its final hardening were felt as a grievous blow by many of his followers.' He had favoured disestablishment before 1914, and had hesitated to join the Selborne Committee in 1917 on that ground, but 'the Archbishops, who were not blind to the advantages of making a poacher head-keeper, replied that they needed someone with precisely those views on the Committee, and Temple agreed to serve'. Iremonger saw this as Temple's initial undoing: by the time the Selborne Report was published, he was describing disestablishment as a 'great calamity'. 'By 1925', Iremonger continued, 'his conversion was complete', for he told his Manchester diocese that in the question of disestablishment the church need take no interest at all; it was a question for the state only. 'This is indeed a hard saying', Iremonger declared. In 1930, when Temple moved for yet another state-and-church committee, he felt obliged to defend his own consistency before the Church Assembly, recalling that the first declaration of Life and Liberty had been that 'effective self-government must be obtained for the Church even at the cost, if necessary, of disestablishment'. He denied that he was radically repudiating that position, but added that 'I wish to add that I have seen more reason since for valuing what is called the Establishment.' In later years he insisted that the initiative in breaking the partnership must come from the state, a position which Iremonger thought meant a denial of the spiritual independence of the church. Iremonger concluded:

However these statements may be reconciled, Temple made no attempt to disguise the complete bouleversement of his earlier convictions . . . he became more and more convinced of the advantages to be gained by the State from its connexion with the Church, and this dominated his thinking to the end. Some of his old colleagues in the Life and Liberty Movement [Iremonger had been one, but it was now 1948] look in vain for another of his calibre and authority to lead a disestablishment movement from within the Church such as once appeared possible – and the Establishment is to be left to rust out. (Iremonger, 1948, pp. 357–9)

For Iremonger Temple was the lost leader of the Life and Liberty generation, almost, in this particular context, a traitor. This judgement seems to me to be unfair as well as inaccurate. It is true that Adrian Hastings, writing in 1986, and from a Roman Catholic point of view, depreciated Temple as 'a man for consensus, for a progressive consensus, and where he could carry a consensus – above all within the newly developing ecumenical circles – he marched cheerfully forward. Where he could not do so because issues were intractable, human divisions too sharp, he shrank instinctively from any sort of sectarian or party leadership, retreating rather within the banal or simply into the pursuit of other causes. He was not a man to be in a minority' (Hastings, 1986, p. 257).

Professor Hastings's portrait of Temple would explain the latter's failure, as Iremonger understood it, to march cheerfully forward in the cause of Anglican 'independence', but does not account for Temple's presence at the front of Life and Liberty, or for his sustained political partisanship (as it certainly seemed to open anti-socialists like Headlam, Henson and Inge), which stretched from Copec to Malvern in what ecclesiastically was always a minority. In the specific case of the relationship between church and state, however, it was Iremonger who missed the point rather than Temple who failed the cause. Life and Liberty was not a campaign to disestablish the Church of England: there were threats – from Charles Gore, for example, as well as Temple – to consider such a campaign if reform was blocked, but the aim of the leaders was to give the laity a share in running the system in the hope (as far as Temple was concerned) of modernising the state church. Once the Assembly existed, with a validly elected House of Laity in place, disestablishment was not a serious option. Between 1930 and 1944 'independence' was no more than a distraction, a clerical way of blaming on the House of Commons the disunity of the Church of England. It was not Temple's fault if the

Church Assembly's first-generation laity turned out to be conservative. Temple was not betraying the cause of disestablishment when he turned in the early 1920s to the creation of Copec, but seeking to give content to the idea, which was also in the 1917 report, that the Church of England should affect people not only as private individuals but in their social relationships as well. It is true that he was offering the Church Assembly, lay as well as clerical, a programme which by and large it did not want and was prepared to reject on social as well as individual grounds, but he was not reflecting a consensus: he was criticising one.

Nor was Temple inconsistent. Although he shared the dismay with which his episcopal colleagues in 1928 faced the fact that Davidson and Lang had badly misread the attitude of politicians towards the establishment, he was not emotionally committed (and I see no reason why he should have been) to either the Anglo-Catholic or the Anglican Evangelical party-line on the correct forms of worship and doctrine. It was the Bishop of Durham, Hensley Henson, something of a touchstone among conservative church historians in recent years, and a defender of an eighteenth-century view of the establishment for most of his career, who changed sides and demanded disestablishment after the Prayer Book defeat. Henson asserted that 'within recent years the State has become effectively secularised, and now, under the fiction of neutrality, undermines the indispensable postulates of the Christian religion' (Henson, 1929, p. 81). In the case of marriage, for example, the state's legislation on divorce had repudiated 'the morality of Christ'. Henson feared 'the ignominious security of a tame Church in a secularised state'. With all respect to Henson, there seems to be no reason why the decline of Christianity should have led the Church of England to repudiate its connexion with the state. What he also feared was the Labour Party's growing influence in the House of Commons.

As a social theologian, Temple preferred to think of the establishment in positive terms as a means of creating, at least in theory, a religious nation. No one seriously supposed that the revised Prayer Book was going to unite the Church of England, let alone the nation: it was not worth the price of disestablishment. Temple's social theology was rooted in the idea that church and state should combine to reflect the overriding purpose of God. Political obedience to the divine is a very ambiguous concept, which can suit the interests of politicians as well as it does those of church leaders, but secular politicians usually feel that they are as well qualified as ecclesiastics to discern the will of God. Chaplains, who bless the political (and military) process at convenient moments, are tolerable, but the constitution of the modern Western state does not usually allow religious institutions any share of power. Alliances like those between church and state in some South American countries do not require establishment.

One's judgement of the legitimacy of a desire by the Church of England to influence politics depends on whether one views Christianity as the uniting, civilising factor in British society, or whether one acts, as Stanley Baldwin did, on the assumption that a political party has to make itself the uniting, civilising force in a modern society, controlling its own mixture of national and religious sentiment. This is not a question which can be answered in terms of Christianity alone, partly because in a plural society there are other sources of religious feeling and ethics, and partly because Christianity does not act as a single political source of influence, but may be thought of as a loose congeries of pressure-groups, not all of which support the same pro-grammes (in sexual ethics, for example, the divergences are ecumenically irreconcilable).

Temple wanted to escape from this institutional pluralism on the Christian side by ecumenical means. He thought that the state ought to accept moral guidance from the Christian tradition, both about social policy and about questions of war and peace, and like Davidson he took what advantage he could of the Anglican episcopal presence in the House of Lords to influence the decision-making process as directly as possible, though it was symptomatic of the underlying distribution of power that his best speech in the House of Lords, his appeal on behalf of the Jews (23 March 1943) had no visible result.

Temple moved a resolution reminding the government of the systematic destruction of the European Jews, who were getting little practical help from the Allied Powers. He pleaded eloquently for more room to be made in Palestine and in Britain itself for refugees. He dismissed as unworthy the argument that Britain could not feed additional people; as for the suggestion that the admission of more Jews would stimulate British anti-Semitism, he thought that the government should be ready to use the BBC to win the sympathy and confidence of the people. Above all he protested against procrastination:

We cannot rest so long as there is any sense among us that we are not doing all that might be done. We have discussed the matter on the footing that we are not responsible for this great evil, that the burden lies on others, but it is always true that the obligations of decent men are decided for them by contingencies which they did not create and very largely by the action of wicked men. The priest and the Levite in the parable were not in the least responsible for the traveller's wounds as he lay there by the roadside and no doubt they had many other pressing things to attend to, but they stand as the picture of those who are condemned for neglecting the opportunity of showing mercy. We at this moment have upon us a tremendous responsibility. We stand at the bar of history, humanity and of God. (HL *Debates*, vol. 126, col. 821)

In the light of how little was done in response to such pressure, the choice of New Testament reference seems cruelly apt.

In situations and actions of this kind Temple struggled to give meaning to the idea of a 'religious establishment' in the very years when the British state was finding control of the religious life of its citizens superfluous. Religious pluralism already existed by 1918, but it was largely a pluralism of Judaism and differing Christian churches, themselves only loosely related to a majority of the population, which paid no great attention to any form of organised religion at all. It was the entry into Britain after 1945 of increasing numbers of people who adhered to non-Christian religions which changed the balance, and slowly compelled the politicians to renew their acquaintance with the politics of religion.

Religious pluralism makes Anglican establishment difficult to defend, though it is clear that some Anglicans would defend it in almost any circumstances. In a recent Anglican study, Church and Politics Today (1985), edited by George Moyser, for example, Peter Cornwell quoted John Habgood, then Archbishop of York, as saying that 'the growth of tolerance [of pluralism] has always depended on a residual sense that there are some things which hold us together as a nation', and Cornwell went on to say that 'the National Church could become both the articulator and supporter of those common values which are present but submerged beneath the free-for-all of the pluralist society' (p. 54). Cornwell's emphasis on 'common values' rather than on common theological dogmas reminds one of the role of the Hanoverian Church of England as a provider of a stabilising civic ethic: in the late twentieth century, however, there is a wide gap between anything which could be called a common ethic and the ethical attitudes of the various religious groups.

Temple also believed that what held the country together in an organic community must include a world-outlook, which in England should at least be organised by the state church, incorporating other Christian styles as far as possible. He was writing at a time when the pressure from non-Christian religious sub-cultures was still slight, and to that extent his attitude in the 1920s was more plausible than that of Cornwell in the 1990s, where the argument comes close to assuming that whatever kind of national feeling or residual folk-religion holds us together is compatible with Anglicanism and should be articulated through the Anglican establishment. Other Christian styles, and other world-views, compete for attention.

The counter-view, that religious establishment and social pluralism can no longer be reconciled, has been put forward trenchantly by another Anglican intellectual, Professor Ninian Smart, in an essay contributed to *Religion, State, and Society in Modern Britain* (Smart, 1989). Professor Smart cut through the whole position defended by Temple: he argued that the Christian church was transnational and should not subordinate itself to national interests; it should be free to offer a critique, inevitably political, of the world as it is from an allegedly transcendent standpoint. Smart rejected the view that the chief function of religious education was to hand on Christian values, a position which Temple always defended and which Smart thought was strengthened by the existence of an established church. Smart advocated the alternative model of education, which 'introduced children to the values of Christianity, and Judaism, and Islam, and scientific humanism and so forth, partly because these are the genuine constituents of our religious scene in Britain, and partly because we are educating children who willy-nilly will be citizens of the world' (p. 388). Politically, Professor Smart attacked the way in which what he called 'soft Christianity', at work in the rituals surrounding the monarchy and the operations of the state, downgraded other world-views, including scientific humanism, which he rightly said was a strong element in the working-class agnosticism which Temple and others had desperately wanted to reduce. Finally, Smart could be interpreted as feeling that the existence of a state church subtly supported the wider, secular 'Establishment' (which he called 'a rather incompetent elite') which dominated Britain and made only token concessions to pluralism. What was needed was a more open, critical and pluralist society in which the different ethnic and religious groups would feel at home.

A final assessment of Temple's significance depends on what one thinks of the British Welfare State, and what one thinks of the idea that a healthy society needs to rest on the foundation of a shared world-view, a set of common values, which might cohere in a state religion. The British version of the welfare state did not last long enough to generate the set of common values which might have defended it. Temple believed (as he wrote to his right-wing Catholic critic, Major Kindersley, on 2 July 1943) that the Beveridge Plan could be administered so as to increase actual liberty, because 'a liberty in which one of the alternatives theoretically open is existence below the level of civilised life is not a real liberty' (F. S. Temple, 1963, pp. 91–2), and he would certainly have given the postwar Attlee government more support than came from his successor, Fisher. The value of that support would have depended on the extent to which Anglicanism itself had been impressed by the Archbishop's Malvern campaign, and by *Christianity and Social Order*: given the social composition of the Church of England, and the developing strength of its Evangelical wing after 1945, one suspects that the attack on the Welfare State always drew warm backing from many in the Church of England.

Temple wanted the concept of a welfare state to become part of the Anglican as well as the British world-view. In his letter to Kindersley he agreed that 'all this planning, which I regard as quite inevitable but also, as an alternative to the condition we have been in for the last thirty years, desirable, will result in servitude [Kindersley had taken the Belloc line about the socialist 'servile state'] unless it is quite consciously what Mannheim describes as "planning for freedom"'. He asserted, however, that Britain, 'which has a peculiar genius for working out in practice the correlation of principles that seem to be logically opposed to each other, may be able to show the world what is not so much a middle path between communism and individualism as a genuine expression of the sound principles lying behind each' (p. 92). Temple, easily tempted into the byways of Anglican romanticism, thought that Anglicanism itself exemplified this 'peculiar genius' and that the mid-twentieth-century Church of England was the result of 'planning for freedom'. Such descriptions of Anglicanism were sure of a warm response, but to identify the Welfare State with Anglican morality and politics was implausible.

The relevance of world-views to a given society has been changed since 1945 by an unstoppable *Völkerwanderung*, which has compelled Western societies to face the possibility that they cannot live on the basis of a shared world-view, but have to tolerate the unreconciled presence of several such systems. At this point events have negated the simple picture of the world which Temple had inherited, in which a divinely ordained British state benefited internally from the unifying and civilising power of the state church, while the world-order gained from the unifying Christian influence of the British Empire. There is a wide gap therefore between Temple's belief in the value of a state church, and the development in Britain of religious pluralism. By 'religion' I mean whatever system of ideas or stories or institutions individual people and groups use in order to give meaning to the universe and their existence in it. Religion defined in this way can hardly die out at the individual level, but it is not so certain that any particular religious system, including the Christian one, is bound to remain plausible, or that a given society must have one dominant civil religion which functions for the society as a whole as a source of common standards.

Indeed, what, by this time, Anglicanism would mean to the nation was no longer clear. When he signed as chairman the carefully balanced report *Doctrine in the Church of England* in 1937, Temple added a formal profession of his own faith:

I think it right here to affirm that I wholeheartedly accept as historical facts the Birth of Our Lord from a Virgin Mother and the Resurrection of his physical body from death and the tomb. And I anticipate, though with less assurance [this was a reversion to the kind of caveat which he had proposed before 1914], that these events will appear to be intrinsically bound up with his Deity when the relations between the spiritual and physical elements in our nature are more completely understood. But I fully recognise the position of those who sincerely affirm the reality of Our Lord's Incarnation without accepting one or both of these events as actual historical occurrences, regarding the records rather as parables than as history, a presentation of spiritual truth in narrative form. (p. 12)

This was a liberal-minded statement. The modernisation and consequently the survival of the state church required in Temple's opinion the toleration of those who did not accept the Virgin Birth and physical Resurrection of Jesus as historical facts, just as it required the toleration of those who, like himself, accepted them as historical events but drew no far-reaching theological conclusions from them. He could envisage doctrinal pluralism more easily than he could envisage religious pluralism. To this extent the report's stress on the toleration of alternative theologies was ahead of its time, but if one were to justify the idea of an 'Anglican nation', one would have had to turn to a broader and less specifically Christian religious outlook of a kind common outside the organised churches but also found among both Anglo-Catholics and Evangelicals. If one examines Temple's occasional references to his own spiritual life, there is clear evidence of this common religion, with its emphasis on the existence of a providential order which governs people's lives, resolves wider conflicts and guarantees a happy ending. In a lecture given in 1968 D. M. MacKinnon criticised Temple by implication as one of those Platonising theologians who had damaged Christianity by inflicting on it Plato's flight from the tragic as the ultimate religious category (in MacKinnon, 1969, pp. 37–40), and so, in our present terms, making this common religion respectable; it would be fairer to say, however, that common religion feeds off orthodox Christianity's inability to cope with the tragic.

In Temple's case traces of this common religion can be seen in his defence of intercessory prayer, the practice of asking for direct supernatural help in everyday matters. In a remarkable sentence in *Christus Veritas* (1924), he said:

When I prayed for the safety of my friends during the Great War I did not suppose that God would deflect bullets in order to save them, but I did and do believe that He might see fit to prompt them to some apparently accidental movement which would save them. The impulse to pray is justified if such a thing is even possible. (pp. 195–6)

This was the standard set of Western religion, fed by a personal need to believe that God responded to appeals for direct action, even if he seemed to do so indirectly. Coincidences and 'apparently accidental movement' have always been an important element of popular religion. He went further than this in *The Kingdom of God* (1914a), saying that

I wish quite definitely to say that whatever our view of specific miracles may be, the demand for miracle is absolutely inherent in religion. Either religion is nothing at all for us, or else it is belief in a power which enables a man to do what without his religion he could not do, that is, to act in ways which the study of natural science will never lead us to understand. What the limits of this new power may be, I do not know. It may include power over perfectly dead matter, or it may not. I am inclined to think that it does, for I believe that faith makes available for man all the infinite resources of Almighty God, so that by faith a man could literally walk on the water or remove mountains . . . (p. 124)

A hedging openmindedness, which did not want to deny the demands of popular religion, was all very well, but there was something unsatisfying in merely inclining to the belief that faith might walk on water. One recognises the grip of other, more specifically Christian factors, such as concern for the declining status of the New Testament text and anxiety about any judgement which placed the reported acts of Jesus outside credibility. This is not entirely in line, however, with the view found in *Christus Veritas* that God might prompt a sideways movement in a man but not a sideways movement in a bullet. There is the same approach through the faith of the individual rather than through the bullet or the water, but in one case the faith (we incline to think) controls the water, and in the other case the faith does not (we incline now to think) grip on the bullet. The confusion suggests a deep personal refusal to abandon feelings which must have been part of his early education in the world of his elderly Victorian father.

Another example of common religion, belief in divine guidance, can be found in an autobiographical passage from one of his addresses to Oxford undergraduates during a

Mission of 1931. Iremonger, rightly as far as one can see, thought that Temple was describing his anxieties about going to Repton as headmaster in 1910:

I had once to make a choice which I found very difficult. I was much interested in the work I was doing, believing it to be of some value. I was asked to take up another post which certainly was more conspicuous in the eyes of the world. I tried to avoid it. I asked all the friends of whom I could think, and they all said that I had better stay where I was. I had to make a decision in time to write a letter by a certain post, and having weighed up the question as carefully as I could – and we must always do that – and having come to no conclusion at all, I began at eight o'clock in the evening to say my prayers, and for three hours, without a pause, I tried to concentrate all my desires on knowing clearly what was God's will for me. I do not know how those three hours went; they did not seem very long; but when eleven o'clock struck I knew perfectly well what I had got to do, and that was to accept; and I have never had a shadow of doubt since that it was right . . . Each man has to find his own vocation. Every man is able to find that out if, quite sincerely, he will seek to do, not his own will, but God's. (Temple, 1931, p. 51)

For all Temple's certainty in 1910, however, and the approval with which he looked back on his decision from Oxford in 1931, at the time he had changed his mind about Repton within about two years, and moved to a central London church with relief in 1914. If he had a vocation it was not to be a headmaster, and his own experience illustrated the weaknesses of the argument that he was using.

There is another good example of this way of describing the alleged relationship between the divine and the human in *Christus Veritas* (1924), where the following passage appeared as a footnote to the claim that 'people who take care to keep their devotional life fresh and vigorous find repeatedly that they are guided to act or speak in ways the value of which is only afterwards appreciated':

Personal testimony is the most appropriate support of such a statement. I have found that at times when I have been taking due trouble about my own devotional life I have frequently felt an unreasoned impulse to go and see some one whom (as it turned out) I was able to help considerably. I have also noticed that if I get slack about my prayers such coincidences cease. Preachers who pray over their sermons often find that some sentence which they doubtfully insert, or utter on the spur of the moment, is exactly calculated to meet the spiritual need of someone in the congregation. (p. 195)

Temple was not always close to the popular mind, as can be seen from another example of his personal piety. It was at the same Oxford Student Mission in 1931 that Temple discussed the problems of religion and sex in terms which were destined to become famous long after he was dead. 'It is to be recognised', he said,

that sex is holy as well as wholesome. It is the means by which we may bring into the world – not only as with the animal creation others of our biological species – it is the means by which we may co-operate with God in bringing into the world children of His own destined for eternal life. Anyone, who has once understood that, will be quite as careful as any Puritan to avoid making jokes about sex; not because it [sex] is nasty, but because it is sacred. He would no more joke about sex than he would joke about the Holy Communion – and for exactly the same reason. To joke about it is to treat with lightness something that deserves reverence. (Temple, 1931, p. 49)

These words were referred to by J. A. T. Robinson in the early 1960s when he testified in court supporting D. H. Lawrence's novel *Lady Chatterley's Lover* against charges of obscenity. In the context of the trial the passage sounded like the epitome of clerical innocence. Robinson did not realise that Temple's words might be interpreted in terms of the Victorian Purity Movement, possibly because he knew that he was quoting from a discussion of moral standards in which Temple had said, over against Victorian attitudes to sex, that 'we have, in a certain sense, to make a new start about this, and begin with the recognition of the complete wholesomeness of the natural fact of sex' (p. 48). Temple's choice of 'wholesomeness' suggested a queasiness about the recognition, but he was talking to students as a former headmaster, and he balanced this assertion with the suggestion that 'it is to be recognised that sex is holy as well as wholesome' (p. 49). Once again the choice of the words grates, because 'holy' and 'wholesome' sound awkward together. In what followed Temple invoked the Holy Communion as a symbol of the 'holy': he was not equating the emotions involved. His real target was promiscuity (and in this sense he might be said to have been on Lawrence's side), but when he said that 'the union of the sexes physically can only be right when it is the expression of a spiritual union of such quality that it is inevitably lifelong' (p. 49), he was also implying a sophisticated defence of the traditional Christian view that marriage was indissoluble. Temple, who habitually repeated himself on these subjects, said the same thing in 1943 to the Church of England Men's Society: 'the reason for not joking about sex is exactly the same as for not joking about the Holy Communion. It is not that the subject is nasty, but that it is sacred, and to joke about it is profanity' (Iremonger, 1948, p. 448).

Between 1870 and 1920 the British mainstream churches increasingly felt that their mid-Victorian combination of orthodox dogma with popular religion had become inadequate. There seemed to be a need to widen the social area to which a 'Christian' meaning had to be given. 'Christianity' as personal salvation no longer worked adequately; the bourgeois individual hero, who stood on his own feet and mastered the visible, could no longer be made acceptable by 'conversion', contributions to charity, and the Protestant work-ethic, though he was to become popular again in the 1980s. Society itself to some extent turned against him and repudiated his position, and Christian intellectuals found themselves arguing, as early as 1850, against the claim that competition was an indefeasible economic law. If this was the case, if one had to believe, for the moment, that the social consequences of laissez-faire had changed the ethical position, and that the language of the New Testament could be used to require greater social equality, for example, then what Temple did was not really 'adaptation', a betrayal of a theological tradition, or the expression of a loss of faith, but a pragmatic extension of religion, at least as far as 'meaning' was concerned. One had for the moment to offer a more comprehensive social account of Christianity, whether or not this culminated in action. From the standpoint of Temple's philosophical idealism this could be interpreted as a belief that one had grasped the inevitable, progressive direction of history. It was for this belief that Karl Popper criticised Mannheim (and by implication the Anglican Moot) in *The Poverty of Historicism* (1957), but, even putting Mannheim and the Zeitgeist firmly on one side, there was still a strong local, temporary historical rationality, founded in the prevailing socio-economic circumstances, in re-examining the relationship between the churches and society.

In the wake of the First Vatican Council (1870) Roman Catholics believed that they had already solved the problems of political modernisation in their own way by creating new institutions within the ecclesia; society should join the church, not the church society. The Catholics wanted to revert to a Rome-centred world by contracting out of the non-Catholic society; there would be Catholic businesses, Catholic trade unions, Catholic recreation clubs, Catholic schools and universities and so on, and all this would be subordinated to the hierarchy in the last resort. This was a deeply pessimistic attitude, according to which the best that could be done was to prevent change, which could only be for the worse. The approach did not work well in England, where Cardinal Manning's would-be university soon collapsed and no separate Catholic trade union congress appeared (as happened in France, for example).

The gap between Roman Catholic and Protestant positions became clear at Copec. The machinery did not exist in the Protestant churches to realise the Catholic vision of a completely withdrawn religious sub-culture within a society. Protestant plurality is supposed to be a sign of Protestant weakness, but may also be seen as willingness to remain in contact with a changing society. Between 1870 and at least 1920 the Protestant reaction depended on the judgement that the working classes had an ethical case to be answered, that free-market capitalism might produce the best economic results, but it was not certain that it produced the best or most ethical society.

Temple lived at a time when in England the formation of a specifically religious political party, though occasionally mentioned, seemed impossible in practice. At the same time, the secularity of British government was hardly affected by the existence of the Church of England, of the Coronation liturgy and of parliamentary legislation about religious matters. His solution was to try to create a political equivalent of the Victorian Missionary Societies, which had been outside direct church control. They had always had political policies in practice, as when, for example, the Missions constantly criticised the administration in India, arguing that Britain should seek to christianise the Indians in order to produce loyal subjects; or when in the twentieth century American and British missions to China committed themselves on the side of the Nationalists. Such institutions were always open to the charge that they wanted power without responsibility,

and the problem surfaced again after 1945 when new bodies
were formed largely concerned with international aid which
often found a conflict developing between their charity
status, which excluded politics, and the need for political as
well as relief solutions in some situations. Temple did not
want a single-issue pressure-group; instead, both in 1924
and again after Malvern he thought in terms of a broad
institution with a permanent secretary and a central committee, preferably with some non-Anglican members; there
would also be local committees, partly for discussion, partly
for raising money.

Temple's solution inevitably failed because he was not
satisfied either with conversions, or with the limited results
of relief work: he wanted political results, and was not
content, as J. H. Oldham or Randall Davidson were, with the
rewards of club diplomacy in Whitehall. This was to be
increasingly the problem of churches which found themselves at odds with society, whether Marxist or market-
capitalist. What Temple was asking for by 1941 was change in
the direction of a social-welfare mixed economy, as is amply
demonstrated in the Penguin Special, *Christianity and Social Order*.
This was a political programme, however one might disguise
the fact by talk about 'middle axioms'. Such a programme
was not suited to single-issue pressure-group methods, like
those used in the 'religious' campaigns of the 1980s against
contraception and abortion, campaigns which could be
staged on an allegedly moral, non-political basis, even
though the aim was legislation which would interfere with
private liberty. Logically, Temple's aims required public
political organisation, and this was foreign to the Victorian
religious society tradition, as well as to the Edwardian
Anglican political tradition. At the time of Copec Temple had
to say that he did not want a separate political party but only
Christian influence in all parties, but in the long run this was

self-contradictory, because the impact of Temple's social ideas fell left of centre. Logically, in a plural society the 'church', if it wants to have political influence (and all mainstream churches do), should commit itself to the organisation of one or more political groups. Whether this is a good thing for the society in which it happens is another question.

Our interpretation of Temple's period is inevitably affected by the way in which the situation changed again later. There was not the steady movement in a progressive direction which the 'New Liberalism' and progressive Anglicanism hoped for. The right fought back with unexpected vigour, and by the 1980s the bourgeois hero had reasserted himself, was boasting about his superior cunning and the virtues of making money; he stood on everyone else's feet and flatly denied the moral and social value of the Welfare State. There was still no question of a 'Christian-democratic' party, but instead religious pressure-groups such as the anti-abortion groups appeared. The right did not object to religious involvement in politics when these groups, which had no overall social programme, appeared with their letter-writing supporters and protesting crowds. The situation in the Christian sub-culture in the late 1970s could be interpreted as conflict between two religious universes of meaning, the 'liberal Anglican' and the 'conservative Evangelical/Catholic'. Temple's vision of a single Christian ideological movement working through the establishment to bring rational pressure to bear on the law-makers had been lost. Churchill, unhappy at having to concede Temple's appointment as Archbishop of Canterbury, allegedly consoled himself by describing Temple as 'the half-crown article in a penny bazaar'. It was a fair description of the gap between the new Archbishop and the old institution.

# References

Davidson Papers, Temple Papers, both in Lambeth Palace Library

The Archbishops' Committee on Church and State: Report. London, SPCK. Cited as Selborne, 1917

Church Assembly, Church and State: Report of the Archbishops' Commission . . . 2 vols., London, Press and Publications Board of the Church Assembly, 1935. Cited as Cecil, 1935

The Church and Industrial Problems, Report of the Archbishops' 5th Commission of Enquiry. London, SPCK, 1918

Church and State: Report of the Archbishops' Commission. London, Church Information Office, 1970. Cited as Chadwick, 1970

Doctrine in the Church of England . . . Report of the Archbishops' Commission. London, SPCK, 1938

Annan, N. 1990. Our Age: The Generation that made Postwar Britain. London, Weidenfeld & Nicolson

Barnett, C. 1986. The Audit of War. London, Macmillan

Barth, K. 1941. A Letter to Great Britain from Switzerland. London, Sheldon Press

Bell, G. K. A. 1935. Randall Davidson. Oxford University Press

Belloc, H. 1912. The Servile State. London, T. N. Foulis

Bennett, G. V. 1975. The Tory Crisis in Church and State, 1688–1730: The Career of Francis Atterbury, Bishop of Rochester. Oxford, Oxford University Press

# References

Berdyaev, Nicholas. 1943. *Slavery and Freedom*. London, Geoffrey Bles

Blackburne, H. W. 1932. *This Also Happened on the Western Front*. London, Hodder & Stoughton

Boegner, M. 1970. *The Long Road to Unity*. London, Collins

Chadwick, O. 1990. *Michael Ramsey*. Oxford, Oxford University Press

Cole, G. D. H. 1917. *Self-Government in Industry*. London, Bell

Conference on Christian Politics, Economics and Citizenship. 1924. *Reports*. 12 vols., London, Longmans

Cornwell, P. 1985. 'The Church of England and the State', in G. Moyser (ed.), *Church and Politics Today*. Edinburgh, T. Clarke, pp. 33–54

Cowling, M. 1971. *The Impact of Labour 1920–24*. Cambridge, Cambridge University Press

Craig, R. 1963. *Social Concern in the Thought of William Temple*. London, Gollancz

Crick, P. C. T. 1921. *The Voice of the Layman and the Church of the Future*. Cambridge, Heffer

Demant, V. A. 1939. *The Religious Prospect*. London, Frederick Muller

Edwards, E. W. 1934. Review of *Nature, Man and God* in *Mind*, New Series, 43

Fletcher, J. 1963. *William Temple: Twentieth-Century Christian*. New York, Seabury Press

Fox, R. W. 1985. *Reinhold Niebuhr*. New York, Pantheon

Freeden, M. 1978. *The New Liberalism, An Ideology of Social Reform*. Oxford, Oxford University Press

   1986. *Liberalism Divided: A study in British Political Thought*. Oxford, Oxford University Press

Harris, J. 1990. 'Enterprise and Welfare States', *Transactions of the Royal Historical Society*, Fifth Series, 40, pp. 175–96.

Hastings, A. 1986. *A History of English Christianity 1920–1985*. London, Collins

Henson, H. H. 1924. *Quo Tendimus, Primary Charge*. London, Hodder & Stoughton

   1929. *Disestablishment*. London, Macmillan

   1942–50. *Retrospect of an Unimportant Life*. 3 vols., Oxford, Oxford University Press

# References

Hobson, J. A. 1927. *The Conditions of Industrial Peace.* London, Allen & Unwin

Holland, H. S. ed. 1912. *The Commonwealth, A Christian Social Magazine.* London, Wells, Gardner, Darton

Hooft, V.'t. 1973. *Memoirs.* London, SCM Press

Inge, W. R. 1930. *The Social Teaching of the Church.* London, Epworth

Ingram, K. 1937. *Christianity – Right or Left?.* London, Allen & Unwin

Iremonger, F. A. 1948. *William Temple Archbishop of Canterbury: His Life and Letters.* Oxford, Oxford University Press

Jackson, E. M. 1980. *Red Tape and the Gospel: A study of . . . William Paton.* Birmingham, Phlogiston/Selly Oak Colleges

Jasper, R. C. D. 1967. *George Bell, Bishop of Chichester.* Oxford, Oxford University Press

Knox, R. A. 1913. *Some Loose Stones.* London, Longman, Green

Kojecky, R. 1971. *T. S. Eliot's Social Criticism.* London, Faber

Loader, C. 1985. *The Intellectual Development of Karl Mannheim, Culture, Politics and Planning.* Cambridge, Cambridge University Press

MacKinnon, D. M. 1969. *The Stripping of the Altars.* London, Collins

Martin, K. 1926. *The British Public and the General Strike.* London, Hogarth Press

Mills, P. and Smith, M. 1987. *Cinema, Literature and Society.* London, Croom Helm

Norman, E. R. 1976. *Church and Society in England 1770–1970.* Oxford, Clarendon Press

Oldmeadow, E. 1942–4. *Francis, Cardinal Bourne.* 2 vols., London, Burns Oates

Oliver, J. 1968. *The Church and Social Order 1918–39.* London, Mowbray

Padgett, J. F. 1974. *The Christian Philosophy of William Temple.* The Hague, M. Nijhoff

Popper, K. 1974. *The Poverty of Historicism.* London, Routledge (1st edn, 1957)

Preston, R. H. ed. 1976. *Christianity and Social Order.* London, Shepheard-Walwyn/SPCK

Reason, W. ed. 1924. *The Proceedings of C.O.P.E.C.* London, Longmans

Reckitt, M. B. ed. 1945. *Prospect for Christendom.* London, Faber & Faber

Roberts, R. E. 1942. *H. R. L. Sheppard: Life and Letters.* London, Murray

# References

Smart, N. 1989. 'Church, Party and State', in P. Badham (ed.), *Religion, State, and Society in Modern Britain*. Lampeter, E. Mellen Press, pp. 381–93

Streeter, B. H. ed. 1914. *Foundations: A Statement of Christian Belief in Terms of Modern Thought*, by Seven Oxford Men. London, Macmillan (1st edn, 1912)

Suggate, A. M. 1987. *William Temple and Christian Social Ethics Today*. Edinburgh, Clark

Tawney, R. H. 1921. *The Acquisitive Society*. London, Bell
　1931. *Equality*. London, Allen & Unwin
　1953. *The Attack and Other Papers*. London, Allen & Unwin

Taylor, A. E. 1917. Review of *Mens Creatrix* in Mind, New Series, 26

Temple, F. S. ed. 1963. *Some Lambeth Letters 1942–1944*. Oxford, Oxford University Press

Temple, W. 1910. *The Faith and Modern Thought*. London, Macmillan
　1913. *Repton School Sermons*. London, Macmillan
　1914a. *The Kingdom of God*. London, Macmillan
　1914b. *Studies in the Spirit and Truth of Christianity*. London, Macmillan
　1915. *Church and Nation*. London, Macmillan
　1917. *Mens Creatrix*. London, Macmillan
　1924. *Christus Veritas*. London, Macmillan
　1931. *Christian Faith and Life*. London, SCM Press
　1934. *Nature, Man and God*. London, Macmillan
　1939–40. *Readings in St. John's Gospel*. 2 vols., London, Macmillan
　1942. *Christianity and Social Order*. Harmondsworth, Penguin. References are to the new edition, ed. R. H. Preston, London, Shepheard-Walwyn/SPCK, 1976
　1945. *Christianity as an Interpretation of History*. London, Longmans
　1958. *Religious Experience*, ed. A. E. Baker. London, James Clarke

Thompson, K. A. 1970. *Bureaucracy and Church Reform: The Organizational Response of the Church of England to Social Change 1800–1965*. Oxford, Oxford University Press

# Index

Acland, R., 130, 157–64, 163
Anglican Evangelicals, 33–4, 163, 179
Anglo-Catholics, 33–4, 62, 64, 80–1, 163

Baldwin, S., 4, 27, 31, 108, 117, 137, 138, 140–6, 175
Balfour, A., 63, 138
Barnett, C., 3, 6–7, 156
Barth, K., 100–3, 109
Bell, C., 132
Bell, Bishop George, 79, 85, 89, 96, 108–11, 157–61, 171
Belloc, H., 120, 152, 180
Bennett, G. V., 36
Berdyaev, N., 131–2
Berggrav, E., 101–2, 107–10
Blackburne, H., 71, 80
Boegner, M., 96, 103, 108–9, 111
Bosanquet, H., 56, 128
Bourne, Cardinal, 136
Butler, R. A., 163

Carter, H., 108–10, 139
Cecil, R., 97, 120
Cecil Report (1935), 168, 169–70
Chadwick Report (1970), 168
*Challenge*, 25, 65–70, 79, 89, 106
Charity Organisation Society, 21, 128
Christendom Group, 149, 151–8, 162, 164, 165
*Christianity and Industrial Problems* (1918), 117–18, 160

Church and State (*see also* Life and Liberty), 33–7, 81–2, 127, 168–79
Churchill, W., 111, 171, 190
Cole, G. D. H., 152
common/popular religion, 64, 177–8, 182–6
Communism, 57–8, 102, 110, 143
Conservative Party, 29, 117, 120, 146, 160, 163
Copec, 115–34
Cornwell, P., 177–8
Creighton, L., 77, 90
Crick, P. C. T., 71

Davidson, Archbishop Randall, 13–14, 31, 61, 67–8, 75–6, 79, 82–95, 123–4, 136–42, 144–5, 169–71, 175
Demant, V. A., 151, 155–6, 162
De Zilven, 108–11
Divinity of Christ, doctrine of, 13–15, 23, 38–46, 181

education, 16–19, 37, 125, 163, 165, 178
Edwards, E.W., 54
Eliot, T. S., 151, 158, 162

Faith and Order, 95, 96, 97, 148
Federal Union, 107
Figgis, J. N., 151

# Index

Franco, General, F., 99, 149
Fry, Elizabeth, 21

Garbett, Archbishop Cyril, 85
General Strike (1926), 27–8, 134–48
Gore, Bishop Charles, 61, 74–5, 80–1, 87, 88, 117, 173

Habgood, Archbishop John, 177
Harris, J., 163
Hastings, A., 17, 30–1, 84, 144, 173
Headlam, Bishop Arthur, 96, 173
Henson, Bishop Herbert Hensley, 27, 62, 75, 78–83, 93, 120, 122, 145, 173, 174
Hinsley, Cardinal Arthur, 111, 112
Hobson, J. A., 147
Hodges, H. A., 156, 158, 162, 163
Holland, S., 12, 63–4
Hooft, Visser't, 97, 100–4, 108–10

Industrial Christian Fellowship, 119, 137, 145
Ingram, K., 157, 161–2, 163
Iremonger, F. A., 12, 41–2, 45, 73, 77–8, 85–6, 88–9, 92–3, 112, 141, 150, 161, 164, 171–3, 184, 186

Jackson, E. M., 102
Jews, Judaism, 102–4, 107, 120, 154, 176–7, 178
Joad, C. E. M., 107

Kempthorne, Bishop John, 117, 119–20, 137, 140, 142–3
Kennedy, S., 119
Kenyon, R., 126, 129
Keynes, J. M., 165–6
Kindersley, Major G., 179–80
Kirk, P. T. R., 137, 139–41, 145, 155, 157, 163, 164
Knox, R., 35–46

Labour, 66–7, 69, 83, 147
Labour Party, 12, 17, 25, 29, 117, 124, 129, 134, 146, 153
Lang, Archbishop Cosmo, 5, 31, 111, 174, 175

'Lansdowne Letter', 106–7, 110
Liberal theology (see also Modernism, Anglican), 23–4, 58–60, 149–50, 188
Life and Liberty Movement, 25, 26, 61, 73–94, 172–3
Life and Work Movement, 95, 97, 98, 112
Lloyd George, D., 72–3, 116, 120, 171

Mackinnon, D. M., 182
Malvern and After (1941), 164–5
Malvern Conference, 32, 131–2, 148–67, 189
Mannheim, K., 132, 151, 156, 163, 180, 187
Mansbridge, A., 76–7, 85, 117, 169
Modernism
    Anglican, 39, 42
    Catholic, 34, 72
Moot, The, 132, 149, 151, 156, 162–3, 187

National Mission, 25, 64–7, 72, 78, 81, 84, 117
Nazism, 100–7, 109
New Liberalism, 12, 29, 147, 190
Newman, J. H., 36, 37, 69
Niebuhr, R., 96, 131
Nonconformity (Free churches), 33, 47, 124, 139, 146
Norman, E. R., 63, 68, 72, 79, 119, 120, 131, 133, 144–5, 151, 161, 164, 165

Oldham, J. H., 96, 105
Oxford Conference on Church, Community and State (1937), 17, 97–9, 112
Oxford Group, 109

pacifism, 22, 50–1, 126, 150
Padgett, J. F., 58
Paget, Bishop Francis, 13
Paton, W., 96, 103, 105, 107–11
Penty, A. J., 151
Pilgrim, The, 120
Pius XII, Pope, 104, 112
Popper, K., 187

# Index

Prayer Book revision (1927–8), 29, 31, 170–1
Protestantism, 30, 113–14, 188

Raven, C., 22, 68, 123, 145
Representative Church Council, 85, 89, 91–3
Repton School, 13, 16, 19, 38, 184
Roberts, R. E., 73
Robinson, J. A. T., 185–6
Roman Catholic Church, 52, 112–14, 115–16, 187–8
Rowntree, S., 141
Royden, M., 80–1, 86

St James's Piccadilly, 16, 24, 26, 88–9, 92
Samuel Report, 135, 140, 143
Selborne Report, 63, 73, 76–7, 84–5, 89, 92, 118–19, 168–72
Sheppard, H. R. L., 22, 73, 77–8, 80, 85, 88, 89
Smart, N., 178–9
Strachey, J. St L., 93–4
Streeter, A., 122
Streeter, H. B., 23, 38, 45
Student Christian Movement, 15, 96, 114
Suggate, A. M., 131, 144–5, 166

Tawney, R. H., 16–18, 24, 117, 132, 148
Taylor, A. E., 50–1
Temple, Beatrice, 9, 24
Temple, Frances, 9, 24

Temple, Archbishop Frederick, 9–11, 13
Temple, F. S., 107, 171, 179–80
Temple, Archbishop William
 *Christianity as an Interpretation of History*, 50
 *Christianity and Social Order* 32, 130, 143, 164–5, 179, 189
 *Christus Veritas*, 26, 182–3, 184
 *Church and Nation*, 18
 *Doctrine in the Church of England*, 43, 181
 *Faith and Modern Thought, The*, 14–15
 *Foundations*, 23–38, 43–6
 *Kingdom of God, The*, 18–22, 183
 *Mens Creatrix*, 25, 44, 46–53, 65, 74, 83
 *Nature, Man and God*, 29, 48, 53–61
 *Readings in St John's Gospel*, 43
 *Repton School Sermons*, 43
Tennant, F. R., 58, 60
Thatcher, M., 117
Thompson, J. M., 23
Thompson, K., 62, 74, 79
*Times, The*, 19, 79, 111

Vidler, A. R., 156, 158, 160–1, 162, 163

Welfare State, 21, 53, 128, 161, 179–80, 190
Workers' Educational Association, 17–18, 76–7, 94
World Council of Churches, 30–1, 96, 98–105, 109–10, 114